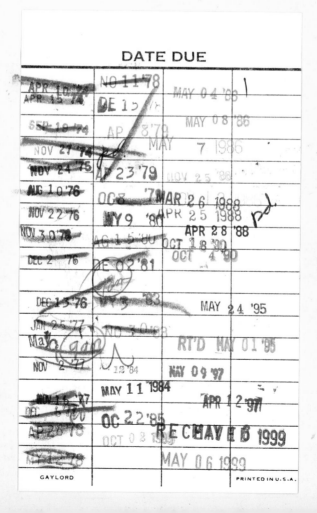

DATE DUE

James Joyce's Early Fiction

JAMES JOYCE'S EARLY FICTION

THE BIOGRAPHY OF A FORM

HOMER OBED BROWN

THE PRESS OF
CASE WESTERN RESERVE UNIVERSITY
Cleveland & London
1972

Library of Congress Cataloging in Publication Data
Brown, Homer Obed, 1933-
    James Joyce's early fiction.
    Includes bibliographical references.
    1. Joyce, James, 1882-1941. I. Title.
PR6019.09Z52634   823'.9'12   72-86350
ISBN 0-8295-0243-2

For Elizabeth and Katharine

Contents

Acknowledgments

A MAJOR PORTION of this book was written while I was supported by grants from the Samuel S. Fels Fund and the Center for Advanced Study at the University of Illinois at Urbana. I wish to thank Dale Phalen of the Fels and David Pines and Betty Yankwich of the Center for their many services. I also wish to thank the many friends and teachers who read and criticized the manuscript and offered encouragement and suggestions for its improvement: Jackson Cope, Earl Wasserman, Eric Solomon, Edgar Dryden, Darcy O'Brien, John Unterecker, William York Tindall, F. W. Dupee, Kenneth Koch, and Edward Said. I owe special debts of gratitude to J. Hillis Miller and to Richard Ellmann for the painstaking care with which they read and commented on the manuscript and to George Stade for his help and encouragement during a difficult period.

For permission to quote from the works of James Joyce I am indebted to the Society of Authors (London), literary representatives of the Joyce Estate, and to the following publishers: in the United States, The Viking Press, Inc. (quotations from *Dubliners*, *A Portrait of the Artist as a Young Man*, Volumes I-III of *The Letters of James Joyce*, and *The Critical Writings of James Joyce*) and New Directions Publishing Corporation (quotations from *Stephen Hero*); in England, Jonathan Cape, Ltd. (quotations from *Dubliners*, *A Portrait of the Artist as a Young Man*, and *Stephen Hero*) and Faber and Faber, Ltd. (quotations from Volumes I-III of *The Letters of James Joyce* and *The Critical Writings of James Joyce*).

I am also grateful to Richard Ellmann for permission to quote from his biography *James Joyce*. Details concerning each of these volumes are given below.

From *The Critical Writings of James Joyce*, edited by Ellsworth Mason and Richard Ellmann. Copyright © 1959 by Harriet Weaver and F. Lionel Monro as administrators of The Estate of James Joyce. All rights reserved. Reprinted by permission of The Viking Press, Inc. and Faber and Faber, Ltd.

From *Dubliners* by James Joyce. Copyright © 1967 by The Estate of James Joyce. Originally published by B. W. Huebsch, Inc. in 1916. All rights reserved. Reprinted by permission of The Viking Press, Inc. and Jonathan Cape, Ltd.

From *James Joyce* by Richard Ellmann, published by Oxford University Press, 1959. Copyright © 1959 by Richard Ellmann. All rights reserved. Reprinted by permission.

From *The Letters of James Joyce*, Volume I, edited by Stuart Gilbert. Copyright © 1957, 1966 by The Viking Press, Inc. All rights reserved. Reprinted by permission of The Viking Press, Inc. and Faber and Faber, Ltd.

From *The Letters of James Joyce*, Volumes II and III, edited by Richard Ellmann. Copyright © 1966 by F. Lionel Monro as administrator of The Estate of James Joyce. All rights reserved. Reprinted by permission of The Viking Press, Inc. and Faber and Faber, Ltd.

From *A Portrait of the Artist As A Young Man* by James Joyce. Copyright © 1964 by The Estate of James Joyce. Originally published by B. W. Huebsch, Inc. in 1916. All rights reserved. Reprinted by permission of The Viking Press, Inc. and Jonathan Cape, Ltd.

From *Stephen Hero* by James Joyce. Copyright © 1943, 1963 by New Directions Publishing Corporation. All rights reserved. Reprinted by permission of New Directions Publishing Corporation and Jonathan Cape, Ltd.

Abbreviations Used

AP   *A Portrait of the Artist as a Young Man,* text corrected from the Dublin holograph by Chester G. Anderson and edited by Richard Ellmann (New York: Viking Compass Books, 1964).

CW   *The Critical Writings of James Joyce,* edited by Ellsworth Mason and Richard Ellmann (London: Faber and Faber, 1959).

D   *Dubliners,* with corrected text by Robert Scholes, in consultation with Richard Ellmann (New York: Viking Compass Books, 1967).

DD   *The Dublin Diary of Stanislaus Joyce,* edited by George Harris Healey (Ithaca, N.Y.: Cornell University Press, 1962).

JJ   Richard Ellmann, *James Joyce* (New York: Oxford University Press, 1959).

Letters   *Letters of James Joyce,* Volume I, edited by Stuart Gilbert, Volumes II & III, edited by Richard Ellmann (New York: Viking Press, 1966).

MBK   Stanislaus Joyce, *My Brother's Keeper: James Joyce's Early Years,* edited, with introduction and notes, by Richard Ellmann (New York: McGraw-Hill Paperback Edition, 1964).

SH   *Stephen Hero*, edited by Theodore Spencer, with additional material edited by John H. Slocum and Herbert Cahoon (Norfolk, Conn.: New Directions Paperbook, 1963).

U   *Ulysses*, new edition, corrected and reset (New York: Modern Library, 1961).

Workshop   *The Workshop of Daedalus: James Joyce and the Raw Materials for* A Portrait of the Artist as a Young Man, collected and edited by Robert Scholes and Richard M. Kain (Evanston, Ill.: Northwestern University Press, 1965).

James Joyce's Early Fiction

Every power in nature
must evolve an opposite
in order to realize itself
and opposition brings
reunion . . .

—Joyce, *Letters*, I, 226.

Introduction

THE POINT OF VIEW of a novel is more than an angle of vision on a
world. Since the action and all people and things of a story are
brought into being by the narrator's words, point of view is also a
certain manner of making things appear. It is a manner of being
which is granted to the world presented. Narrative form is the
structure of a fictional world. The point of view thereby becomes
part of the meaning of that world. It is not my intention to debate
the universality of this proposition. Rather, the value of this approach to point of view will depend here on its usefulness as a
tool for understanding the narrative form of James Joyce's early
fiction. I shall try to show the relationship between that form and
the meaning of the world it presents, and the changes registered
in both the form and the meaning in the development of Joyce's
fiction. His early realist method in *Dubliners* and *Stephen Hero*,
a method that carries its own assumptions about the nature of
reality, is transformed into something new in *A Portrait of the Artist as a Young Man*, and—although my argument ends with the
early work—in *Ulysses* and *Finnegans Wake*. I am concerned with
the way formal development of the early work makes possible the
later evolutions in style.

The relevance of my conception of point of view is indicated
by Joyce's own awareness of such a relationship between point of
view and meaning. In a review in 1903 of the novels of A. E. W.
Mason, Joyce commented: "The novels, much as they differ in
their subjects and styles, are curiously illustrative of the truth of

3

Leonardo's observations. Leonardo, exploring the dark recesses of consciousness in the interests of some semipantheistic psychology, has noted the tendency of the mind to impress its own likeness upon that which it creates" (*CW*, 130).[1]

Joyce did not think of his art as reality copied in a way that would render form neutral and impersonal. In his early notes on Aristotle, he wrote: "*e tekhne mimeitai ten physin*—This phrase is falsely rendered as 'art is an imitation of nature.' Aristotle does not here define art; he says only 'art imitates Nature' and means that the artistic process is like the natural process" (*CW*, 145). This "natural process" is implied in Stephen Dedalus' idea of "artistic conception, artistic gestation, and artistic reproduction" (*AP*, 209), and in the statement that "in the virgin womb of the imagination the word was made flesh" (*AP*, 217). The aesthetic process is a movement of the self toward a realization of itself and a knowledge of itself, as when Joyce, in describing a poem he liked, said "it seems to come out of a personal life which has begun to realize itself" (*CW*, 87). This aspect of the process is suggested by Stephen's conception of a necessary progression of artistic forms:

> The lyrical form is in fact the simplest verbal vesture of an instant of emotion, a rhythmical cry such as ages ago cheered on the man who pulled at the oar or dragged stones up a slope. He who utters it is more conscious of the instant of emotion than of himself as feeling emotion. The simplest epical form is seen emerging out of lyrical literature when the artist prolongs and broods upon himself as the centre of an epical event and this form progresses till the centre of emotional gravity is equidistant from the artist himself and from others. The narrative is no longer personal. . . . The esthetic image in the dramatic form is life purified in and reprojected from the human imagination. (*AP*, 214–15)

This passage has been quoted so often and for so many purposes that quoting it again requires some explanation. My purpose is not to establish a set of pigeonholes for Joyce's works, but to single out a "natural process" which moves from the unself-conscious feelings of the artist through a brooding upon the self "as the centre" to a mediate relationship between the self and the other and finally to an idea of the image "in immediate relation to others" (*AP*, 214). This work will investigate a portion of that process in Joyce's own fiction. It will attempt, again in Joyce's own words, "to establish the relations which . . . subsist between the literary image, the work of art itself, and that energy which had imagined and fashioned it, that centre of conscious, re-acting, particular life, the artist" (*SH*, 77).

The formal development of Joyce's books, when they are regarded in sequence, suggests a changing concept of the nature of reality. Part One of this work focuses on the realism of the early stories of *Dubliners* and pursues the meaning which that realism has. Joyce first planned the book as a complete unit without the long story he finally wrote for its ending, "The Dead." This remained his plan for a long time. If he had suffered less trouble with his publisher, *Dubliners* would have appeared this way. The nature of the book in this form, without "The Dead," is explored in an effort to discover some essential characteristics of the narrator's relationship to his world, as that relationship creates a world. The realism of the *Dubliners* stories implies a dualistic split between observer and observed, spirit and matter, mind and body. The world, inert and despiritualized—"out there"—imprisons a bodyless spirit, a way of seeing. This split is implicit in the form of the work but stated in Stephen's theory of the epiphany. I have tried to capture the basic quality of this particular experience of a world as it existed before Joyce conceived of the transformation of it in "The Dead."

Part Two goes on to the fragmentary *Stephen Hero*, which is contemporaneous with the stories of *Dubliners*. I have tried to show the relationship between these two books and to reveal the similarities in their structures. At the same time that the young Joyce was a cold and distant observer of a dead world, he played the role of a symbolist poet and sought spiritual transcendence. This posing was captured in the somewhat defective mirror of *Stephen Hero*. Part One dealt with a split between narrator and world with an emphasis on the world; this part is concerned with the character of the narrator. The failure of *Stephen Hero* points up the contradictions in Joyce's initial concept of reality.

The writing of "The Dead" signals the emergence of those contradictions into consciousness. Between early 1906, when Joyce's initial plan for *Dubliners* had been fulfilled, and late 1907, when he wrote "The Dead," his thinking had developed beyond his earlier assumptions. There were "changes of heart" about Dublin and an uneasiness about the implications of his stories which are revealed in his letters; moreover, ideas present and developing all along came to the surface, but, most important, the distance in time and the process of writing itself revealed their own truths.

When he wrote "The Dead" in September, 1907, Joyce provided a new ending for *Dubliners* which reflects a basic change of attitude toward the relationships the book suggests. Not only does "The Dead" conclude *Dubliners* but, in another sense, it also concludes *Stephen Hero*, since it was while writing the story that Joyce decided to abandon the old plan for his novel, conceived of the plan he was to follow in *A Portrait of the Artist as a Young Man*, and began to think of its sequel, *Ulysses*.

I do not mean to imply that either *Dubliners* or *Stephen Hero* is limited to the tendencies I discuss. *Dubliners* is a varied work; I limit myself to discussion of the implications of its realism. *Stephen Hero* is a large, lumpy effort which is probably more sophisticated and yet less unified than I give it credit for being. Again, it is a single general tendency that I outline in my discussion of the book. In general, the dialectical process I try to reveal is probably looser in reality than my critical prose will allow, but nowhere do I mean to suggest that Joyce was completely a prisoner of such a scheme. What I am dealing with is the general outline of the progression of his writing.

My final chapter deals with *A Portrait*, which reveals Joyce's new awareness of the implications of the structure of *Dubliners* and *Stephen Hero*. I analyze *A Portrait* to reveal the changes in concept it represents and attempt to show the way it prepares for the later work. The process, then, which is brought to light in this study is a moment in the development of a "life which has begun to realize itself." It is the beginning of a biography of a form.

Part of that biography is founded upon what Joyce learned in the process of writing. The biography of Joyce's particular forms is part of the biography of the novel in general. Joyce discovered, I think, truths that are implicit in the form of fiction and problematic for the novel from its beginning.

In the first place, probably the reason it is difficult to assign a beginning to the novel as a genre is that the novel was never truly "novel"; that is to say, from the first it was predicated on the previous existence of a literary fiction that had betrayed experience and alienated the mind from "reality," e.g., *Don Quixote*. Yet, the novel's own nature as a book doomed it to the same betrayal it sought to escape. Borges' "Parable of Cervantes and Don Quixote" points to the paradox:

> For both of them, for the dreamer and the dreamed, the tissue of that whole plot consisted in the contraposition of two worlds: the unreal world of the books of chivalry and the common everyday world of the seventeenth century.
> Little did they suspect that the years would end by wearing away the disharmony. Little did they suspect that La Mancha and Montiel and the knight's frail figure would be, for the future, no less poetic than Sinbad's haunts or Ariosto's vast geographies.
> For myth is at the beginning of literature, and also at its end.[2]

Joyce had started out to expose the spiritual death of a world he felt was alien to his own nature. By the time he had conceived of "The Dead," Joyce knew he was not Stephen (on the night of June 16, 1904, when Joyce had Stephen wandering drunkenly through Nighttown, Joyce himself had been with Nora Barnacle), and he knew also that the world which had seemed separate from him, "out there," was *his* world, part of him as he was inextricably part of it. "The Dead" explores the possibilities of this discovery as it questions the unspoken assumptions of the narrator of the earlier stories, assumptions incarnated in Gabriel Conroy, and so transforms the nature of the book. At the end of "The Dead," the barriers between Gabriel and the seemingly fixed world outside him dissolve as he realizes his oneness with it. The end of "The Dead" looks forward to the form of *A Portrait*, which Joyce was planning as he wrote that ending—a form which at once presents Stephen's experience as an alienated observer of the world around him and at the same time denies that separation, since we see the world in that novel as it is present in Stephen's mind. (At the same time, however, this apparently subjective form reveals the "truth" about both Stephen and his world.) The end of "The Dead" also anticipates Stephen's at-one-ment with Bloom at the end of *Ulysses*. Finally, it looks ahead also to the fluidity of *Finnegans Wake*, in which each character is constantly dissolving into another, that dream of a man who is everyone simultaneously. The simplest way of describing the dialectical process of Joyce's writing is the rather Hegelian explanation Joyce gave of his use of the philosophy of Giordano Bruno, in a letter to Harriet Shaw Weaver: "His philosophy is a kind of dualism—every power in nature must evolve an opposite in order to realize itself and opposition brings reunion . . ." (*Letters*, I, 226).

The difficult part is to understand and demonstrate how Joyce was able to steer clear of the Charybdis of idealism (Stephen toys with Berkeleyan notions in *Ulysses*, Shem is confused with and by Berkeley in *Finnegans Wake*) as he had earlier avoided the Scylla of realism. The answer, I think, lies in the complicated theories of language and fiction that Joyce developed: he came to see language and fiction as being more originative of reality than representative of it. The early Stephen had begun as a disguise for Joyce, yet turned out to be a fiction. *A Portrait* begins, "Once upon a time . . . ," and Stephen's reality is thoroughly mediated if not originated by the fictions he takes for reality. Each episode goes from an order realized as a fiction through a chaotic awakening in the form of a fall (both of which are constant motifs in the book) to the institution of a new order. *Ulysses* juxtaposes a contemporary, ordinary reality with an ancient mythic fiction, and each episode represents one of the ways mind attempts to order reality and capture its truth: journalism, oratory, musical form, the saga, drama, the penny novel, the historic development of language itself, stream of consciousness. Yet each of Stephen's fictions, each distorting point of view, reveals a truth about experience at the same time that it hides it. The penny-novel parody of Gertie McDowell's mind is both true to her experience and reveals a truth about that experience; moreover, it shows another aspect (as true as any other) of Bloom. In the Nighttown episode, the "insides" and "outsides" of the characters' minds exist on the same level and are intermingled. What would seem to be the most subjective moment of the book, when Stephen communes with Bloom, takes place among the figures and facts and catalogues of objects in the Ithaca episode. The most "subjective" moment of the book in terms of novelistic form, however, is its last, when all the previous narrators have withdrawn and we are thrown completely into the flow of Molly's mind, yet Joyce intended us to grasp this as the most material, "objective" thing of all: "I have rejected the usual interpretation of her as a human apparition—that aspect being better represented by Calypso, Nausicaa and Circe, to say nothing of the pseudo Homeric figures. In conception and technique I tried to depict the earth which is prehuman and presumably posthuman" (*Letters*, I, 180).

Some sense can be made of these paradoxes by understanding Joyce's ideas about language. Words, like the human body (which, as Joyce's chart, letters, and other comments reveal, is the model for *Ulysses*), are both thing and thought, and Joyce saw the artist as investing a dead language with new thought, just as a priest calls back the incarnation of the divine presence in the Eucharist during the Mass.

Joyce goes further in *Finnegans Wake*. Because mind is a matrix of all possible incarnations of the human spirit in all possible and past myths and stories, and in all possible selves, the book is a dream containing all of history and every identity is endless metamorphosis. Here Joyce created a language into which all languages are condensed, a primordial dream language always at the point of dissolution, which at once mimics the multiplicity of experience, "represents" it, and yet creates it anew. The dream of pure archetypal form incarnating by a necessary synecdoche all possible meanings: "I, entelechy, form of forms . . ."

The work of James Joyce provides the perfect means of investigating the philosophical implications of the form of the novel, literary form in general, and perhaps the nature of language itself. His work touches upon all the themes and problems of modernism and crosses the paths of many different contemporary writers. Like Conrad and others, he conceived of literature as something like a lie by means of which one could expose an otherwise elusive truth. Like Lawrence, Joyce shed old selves and dead truths and sought the new through the dialectics of writing.

NOTES

1. Joyce repeats this idea in his early essay on James Clarence Mangan: "There is a likeness between the desperate writer, himself the victim of too dexterous torture, and the contorted writing" (*CW*, 78).
2. *Dreamtigers*, trans. Mildred Boyer and Harold Morland (Austin: University of Texas Press, 1964), p. 42.

I
Division

Chapter One

The Artist as Passive Observer

THE EARLY RECEPTION of James Joyce's *Dubliners* as no more than a realistic picture of contemporary Irish life still holds an important truth and one that, if pursued, will reveal an important key to the development of his fictional world. The more recent emphasis on the symbolism of these stories tends to obscure the way they differ in both form and theme from *Ulysses*, while an understanding of their symbolic "depth," however important, in no way cancels out this surface realism. The universal application of a single principle to describe all of Joyce's works ignores important distinctions among them. Stephen Dedalus' much-quoted formula, for example, of the artist-god who "remains within or behind or beyond or above his handiwork, invisible, refined out of existence, indifferent, paring his fingernails" (*AP*, 215) is revealing when applied to *Dubliners*, but not so helpful with the later works. The area I propose to examine, while it aims to correct this imbalance in the discussion of Joyce's early fiction, is no less singleminded and admittedly does not do justice to the variety of Joyce's work.

The realism of *Dubliners* assumes a world divided between observer and observed. On the one hand is the world of facts, things, and meanings; on the other is the impersonal mind of the observer, passive and watchful. Truth exists out there, independent of me and my knowledge of it. My distance, my separation from the world, is a measure of the validity of my observation. Objectivity consists in the world's otherness. On one side, independent, autonomous things, and other people as things; on the opposite side, pure consciousness, spirit, the passively mirroring self. Between them, distance.

In *Dubliners* there is a double passivity: the paralysis out there is reflected in the passivity of the narrator. The greater the claim for accuracy, the greater must be the passivity of the narrator-mirror. If the picture he presents is completely accurate, he is apparently reduced to being the mere medium of a truth that exists outside. In *Dubliners* both the passivity of the narrator and the paralysis of the characters stem from the original idea of the independence and separateness of things. For example, the opening of "Eveline":

> She sat at the window watching the evening invade the avenue. Her head was leaned against the window curtains and in her nostrils was the odour of dusty cretonne. She was tired.
>
> Few people passed. The man out of the last house passed on his way home; she heard his footsteps clacking along the concrete pavement and afterwards crunching on the cinder path before the new red houses. (*D*, 36)

The window separating observer and observed is an especially revealing motif in *Dubliners*. In this passage, as elsewhere in the book, it emphasizes the character's passivity, paralysis in the face of things over which one has no power. "Her head was leaned" and "in her nostrils was the odour": all possibility of action on her part has been removed. The series of details, separately given, apparently autonomous, stresses her passivity. Events are unrelated, without consequence. Each sentence is a new beginning, a separately observed, separately recorded datum in the narrator's experience as well as in Eveline's, whose fatigued, dull thought processes the prose imitates. The sentences are short and strung together loosely without the subordination which would express relation.

On a broader level, the book, consisting of unrelated stories, has the same structure. Joyceans have generally emphasized the book's tight, symbolic organization at the expense of its immediate effect on the reader. It is, after all, a collection of short stories, fragmentary lives without apparent connection with each other. One story ends, another begins. The immediate impression is one of discontinuity. This impression is reinforced by the fact that each story seems to have no beginning and simply trails off at the end. One can argue that the passage just quoted is not a series of fragments because it has a unity of tone or feeling. That unity, however, is the result of the discontinuity. It is the tone of pathos, endurance, the sufferance of a hopeless passivity and helplessness. The "tight structure" of the whole book is based on the same principle.

This pattern is repeated on the level of syntax and paragraph structure throughout the book. Often the broken design is the rhythm of a character's thoughts, but often it is also that of the narrator who is reduced to passivity by what he mirrors. Look, for example, at the way Little Chandler's disconnected rhythm is taken over by the narrator:

> Little Chandler's thoughts ever since lunch time had been of his meeting with Gallaher, of Gallaher's invitation and of the great city London where Gallaher lived. He was called Little Chandler because, though he was but slightly under the average stature, he gave one the idea of being a little man. His hands were white and small, his frame was fragile, his voice was quiet and his manners were refined. He took the greatest care of his fair silken hair and moustache and used perfume discreetly on his handkerchief. The half-moons of his nails were perfect and when he smiled you caught a glimpse of a row of childish white teeth. (*D*, 70)

These are the narrator's words, not Little Chandler's thoughts. Though the simple parallelism of the items in the first sentence captures the workings of Little Chandler's mind, it does so by fragmenting what was a loosely connected but continuous train of thought in the previous paragraph. But the organization of the whole paragraph follows the same loose, associative pattern. The first sentence *loosely* connects it with the previous paragraph. The second sentence picks up the name and sets out in a new direction to explain it. The third sentence begins by reinforcing that explanation with physical details but is sidetracked by a reference to the refinement in his manners. The last two sentences pursue that idea but come back to physical details that are not really related to manners, and yet at the same time the total effect is that this person has been summed up. The reader has been told all he needs to know about him. If the whole description is a unified picture of Little Chandler's childishness, such a unity is again based on the paragraph's discontinuity, or perhaps more precisely, on its loose, simple, inconsequential continuity.

This passivity on the part of both the observer and the observed is a mark of the alienation suffered by both.[1] The form of these stories expresses a relationship of separation already established. In truth, Joyce's realism and alienation are so much the same thing that it is impossible to say that one causes the other. For example, the cool accuracy with which the boy-narrator of "The Sisters" reports the conversation about the death of the priest is the measure of his own apparent detachment:

> "Well, so your old friend is gone, you'll be sorry to hear."
> "Who?" said I.
> "Father Flynn."
> "Is he dead?"
> "Mr Cotter here has just told us. He was passing by the house."
> I knew that I was under observation so I continued eating as if the news had not interested me. (*D*, 10)

This news of a friend's death is expected to affect the boy, but the most he feels is contained in the bland word "interested." The most he feels later, after he is alone, seems to be anger at old Cotter for alluding to him as a child (*D*, 11). His realism is his detachment from the world outside. But, of course, he is deeply disturbed, as the dream and fact of the story reveal. He conceals his interest from those around him, just as the omniscient narrator of the later stories conceals his subjectivity. By hiding his interest from the world, the boy also has apparently hidden it from himself. By separating his feelings from things, he seems by the same stroke to have separated them from himself, which is perhaps his curious way of splitting and making parallel the lack of feeling in himself and in the external world: "I found it strange that neither I nor the day seemed in a mourning mood" (*D*, 12). Instead, the "sensation of freedom" he feels is just that separation and distance from all the things that involve, engage, commit a person to his world.

Many of the progressive revisions in the three versions of this story that we have reveal a tendency on Joyce's part to give distance and objectivity to his narrative by making the point of view less immediate.[2] One of the major changes was to give the narrative distance in time: the narrator is looking back on a past experience, as if trying to understand its meaning, an attempt which in itself expresses a separation from its immediate life. Most of the details reinforce such a separation. For example, the boy is living with people who are only distantly related, an aunt and uncle, foster parents (one of Stephen Dedalus' fantasies of separation).[3] He hides his own thoughts from them and at the same time he does not understand their allusions to the old priest and cannot allow himself to ask about it. He is so cut off from their world that it must remain a mystery to him. In fact the story (and consequently the whole book) opens with what I have described as an emblem of separation—the boy peering at the priest's lighted window, reading its meaning. And the meaning of the priest's illness is abstracted from its context of real pain and suffering. The word "paralysis" is what becomes important to the boy: "But now it sounded to me like the name of some maleficent and sinful being" (D, 9).

The first-person narrator as a detached observer is used in all the stories of *Dubliners*. What is implicit in the narration of a story like "Ivy Day in the Committee Room" is made explicit in "The Sisters." In "The Sisters" the reader can see the observer in the act of observation. This detached observer is perhaps the most fundamental aspect of Joyce's earliest fiction. The Stephen of both *Stephen Hero* and *A Portrait of the Artist as a Young Man* is cut off from his world in the same way as is the first-person narrator in "The Sisters." The fact that they are so much alike has led some readers to say that Stephen is the narrator of the first three stories of *Dubliners*,[4] and it is true that when "The Sisters" first appeared as a story in the *Irish Homestead*, it was signed "Stephen Daedalus."

Both the passive observer-narrator of *Dubliners* and the world he observes are brought together in this passage from *Stephen Hero*:[5]

> //Nearly every day Stephen wandered through the slums watching the sordid lives of the inhabitants. He read all the street-ballads which were stuck in the dusty windows of the Liberties. He read the racing names and prices scrawled in blue pencil outside

the dingy tobacco-shops, the windows of which were adorned with scarlet police journals. He examined all the book-stalls which offered old directories and volumes of sermons and unheard-of treatises [for] at the rate of a penny each or three for twopence. He often posted himself opposite one of the factories in old Dublin at two o'clock to watch the hands coming out to dinner—// principally young boys and girls with colourless, expressionless faces, who seized the opportunity to be gallant in their way. He drifted in and out of interminable chapels in which an old man dozed on a bench or a clerk dusted the woodwork or an old woman prayed before the candle she had lighted. As he walked slowly through the maze of poor streets he stared proudly in return for the glances of stupid wonder that he received and watched from under his eyes the great cow-like trunks of police constables swing slowly round after him as he passed them. These wanderings filled him with deep-seated anger and whenever he encountered a burly black-vested priest taking a stroll of pleasant inspection through these warrens full of swarming and cringing believers he cursed the farce of Irish Catholicism: an island [whereof] the inhabitants of which entrust their wills and minds to others that they may ensure for themselves a life of spiritual paralysis. (*SH*, 145–46)

The "deep-seated anger" that fills Stephen as observer hides behind the impersonal manner of the stories of *Dubliners*.

It is a truism by now that Stephen's epiphanies are also mostly revelations of the paralysis that is one of the themes of *Dubliners*. The epiphany which is used to introduce Stephen's theory is of a scene taking place "on the steps of one of those brown brick houses which seem the very incarnation of Irish paralysis" (*SH*, 211). Much has been said about the technique of the epiphany, which unites *Stephen Hero*, *Dubliners*, and *A Portrait*. What connects the epiphanies and the stories of *Dubliners* with the sordid little scenes Stephen records in *A Portrait* and its early version (scenes which are often taken from Joyce's collection of epiphanies) is that in each case they represent an external scene captured by a silent, detached observer.

Actually, Stephen's division of the epiphany, defined as "a sudden spiritual manifestation," into two basic kinds reveals this same dualism and the spiritual superiority of the observing mind. On the one side there is the revelation of "vulgarity of speech or of gesture," that is to say, vulgarity in an external scene. On the other side is the epiphany of "a memorable phase of the mind itself" (*SH*, 211). What is observed of the outside world is "vulgar"; what takes place in the mind of the observer is "memorable." As Robert Scholes has noted, "The assumption that the observer . . . is superior to his environment is built into the concept itself."[6]

Stephen at his sister's funeral provides an example of the observer's superiority. Not only do we get his observation of "the inexpressibly mean way in which his sister . . . [was] buried" (*SH*, 165) but also his view of another funeral "of someone of the poor class" (*SH*, 167) that precedes it:

> The first funeral went in through the gates where a little crowd of loungers and officials were grouped. Stephen watched them pass in. Two of them who were late pushed their way viciously through the crowd. //A girl, one hand catching the woman's skirt, ran a pace in advance. The girl's face was the face of a fish, discoloured and oblique-eyed; the woman's face was square and pinched, the face of a bargainer. The girl, her mouth distorted, looked up at the woman to see if it was time to cry: //the woman, settling a flat bonnet, hurried on towards the mortuary chapel. (*SH*, 167)

But this little scene is the epitome of the larger one in which it is contained. Both this epiphany and Isabel's funeral are presented as the meticulously recorded observations of a nonparticipant who is able fully to see the falsity and banality of an empty, convention-bound scene. Stephen stands aside and watches.

The same pattern is carried over in the final version of the novel. In Chapter 2 Stephen "chronicled with patience what he saw, detaching himself from it and testing its mortifying flavour in secret." This is followed by three separately recorded little epiphanies, unrelated except by the fact that each of them begins with the phrase "He was sitting . . . ," which emphasizes the passivity of the observer (*AP*, 67–68). The last of these scenes connects the detachment of the observer with his loneliness and isolation:

> He was sitting in the midst of a children's party at Harold's Cross. His silent watchful manner had grown upon him and he took little part in the games. The children, wearing the spoils of their

crackers, danced and romped noisily and, though he tried to share
their merriment, he felt himself a gloomy figure amid the gay
cocked hats and sunbonnets. (*AP*, 68)

Behind each of these examples are dualistic assumptions: the
notion of an external reality and a truth accessible only to a mind
detached from that reality, a mind which neither participates in
nor is like the scene it observes. One description of Stephen in
particular captures an essential quality of this dualism of observer
and observed. Stephen is at the theater: "He was alone at the
side of the balcony, looking out of jaded eyes at the culture of
Dublin in the stalls and at the tawdry scenecloths and human dolls
framed by the garish lamps of the stage" (*AP*, 226). Here the
usually precise details give way to the general category that most
of these scenes fall into: "the culture of Dublin," which is a way of
stating the subject of *Dubliners*. The observing Stephen is alone,
cut off from the rest both by distance and height, "at the side of
the balcony," and also by his attitude of forced passivity, "looking
out of jaded eyes." The metaphor of the theatrical spectacle underlies the cold detachment of Stephen's epiphanies. Places and people are reduced to "tawdry scenecloths and human dolls framed
by the garish lamps of the stage." The kind of paralysis depicted
in *Dubliners* turns men and women into something very like "human dolls."

In one sense, the division between the narrator and his world
was much more pronounced in the earliest version of these stories.
Most of the revisions of the omnisciently narrated stories consist
in closing the distance between the language of the narrator and
the thoughts of the characters, with increased detachment as the
result.[7]

Not only is the division basic to *Dubliners* and the alienation it
suggests the subject of *Stephen Hero* and *A Portrait*, it is also revealed. in Joyce's earliest literary methods. On the one hand is the
dreamy young poet who was in his last years in Belvedere College,
according to his brother Stanislaus, collecting his poems under the
general title *Moods*, significant for its expression of subjectivity.
"It was," wrote Stanislaus, "evidence of the struggle to keep the
spirit within him alive in the midst of all-pervading squalor and
disintegration" (*MBK*, 85). (One of these "moods" was the poem

Joyce has Stephen write in both *Stephen Hero* and *A Portrait*, "Villanelle of the Temptress.")

But on the other hand Joyce is, at the same time, the patient, detached chronicler of a tawdry spectacle, who like the narrator of *Dubliners* effaces his subjectivity in the observation of an external reality. Stanislaus has reported one of the earliest and purest examples of this tendency of the young Joyce:

> But more indicative of the trend of his thoughts were the sketches that he began to write while still at school. . . . He called them *Silhouettes* from the first sketch, and though I remember only two of them there may have been a few more. *Silhouettes*, like the first three stories of *Dubliners*, was written in the first person singular, and described a row of mean little houses along which the narrator passes after nightfall. His attention is attracted by two figures in violent agitation on a lowered window-blind illuminated from within, the burly figure of a man, staggering and threatening with upraised fist, and the smaller sharp-faced figure of a nagging woman. A blow is struck and the light goes out. The narrator waits to see if anything happens afterwards. Yes, the window-blind is illuminated again dimly, by a candle, no doubt, and the woman's sharp profile appears accompanied by two small heads, just above the window-ledge, of children wakened by the noise. The woman's finger is pointed in warning. She is saying, "Don't wake Pa." (*MBK*, 90)

The fact that this is a "silhouette" emphasizes the externality of the description, frames the scene as if on a stage, and exaggerates its distance from the narrator. It presents the voyeuristic aspect of the detached observer in its simplest form. This "silhouette" also underlines the meaning of the window motif as it appears in *Dubliners*.

The self-effacement of the passively observing narrator takes place by stages in *Dubliners*. The book begins with an anonymous first-person narrator, a foster child, at some distance from the world he describes. The omniscient narrator of the later stories seems almost progressively withdrawn behind an icy irony. The greater and more paralyzed the reality, the more withdrawn the narrator. Erich Heller has remarked about the great nineteenth-century realist novelists that "even the 'reality' of the person who does the writing becomes a hateful obstacle to the ultimate ratio-

nal and aesthetic triumph. If only the human subject could be reduced to nothing but seeing, understanding, and writing; if only
the real object could be transmuted into nothing but words."[8]
Whether Heller is right or not about his writers, this goal seems to
be Joyce's in *Dubliners*. The narrator, anonymous in the beginning,
becomes invisible. This movement may be the meaning of the note
in the Trieste notebook: "At times as he walked through the
streets of Dublin he felt that he was really invisible" (*Workshop*,
95). This motif reappears in *Ulysses* in Turko the Terrible's song:
"I am the boy / That can enjoy / Invisibility" (*U*, 10). Also in the
Trieste notebook is the statement: "He desired not to be a man of
letters but a spirit expressing itself through language" (*Workshop*, 96). The narrative mode of *Dubliners* seems an attempt to
reduce the narrator to a function, a disembodied observer, a sensitive organ, or a pure spirit.[9]

NOTES

1. Harry Levin describes the alienation implicit in the form of these
   stories in this way: "The author merely watches, the characters are
   merely revealed, and the emphasis is on the techniques of exposure.
   Realism had already established the artist as an observer; natural-
   ism made him an outsider" (*James Joyce: A Critical Introduction*,
   rev. ed. [Norfolk, Conn.: New Directions Paperbook, 1960], p. 30).
2. See Marvin Magalaner, *Time of Apprenticeship: The Fiction of
   Young James Joyce* (London: Abelard-Schuman, 1959), pp. 82–
   83, 93.
3. *AP*, 98. This passage is especially illuminating for the family situation of the narrator of "The Sisters" and "Araby": "He saw clearly
   too his own futile isolation. He had not gone one step nearer the
   lives he had sought to approach nor bridged the restless shame
   and rancour that divided him from mother and brother and sister.
   He felt that he was hardly of the one blood with them but stood to
   them rather in the mystical kinship of fosterage, fosterchild and
   fosterbrother."
4. For example, Marvin Magalaner and Richard M. Kain, *Joyce:
   The Man, the Work, the Reputation* (New York: Collier Books,
   1962), p. 82. See also Magalaner's *Time*, p. 83.
5. Theodore Spencer's representation of the text will be followed in

all quotations from *Stephen Hero*. Brackets indicate words crossed out or changed. The emendations immediately follow the bracketed words. In the manuscript there are also slashed strokes in red or blue crayon in Joyce's hand beside, under, or across certain phrases, sentences, and paragraphs. These marks are indicated in my text by two diagonal marks on either side of the words marked by Joyce. Although Mr. Spencer feels these marks indicated Joyce's dissatisfaction with the passages, this assumption seems uncertain, since some passages so marked appeared later in *AP*. Spencer adds that "the slashes are made very broadly as if in haste or impatience, so that it is not always easy to decide where, in Joyce's mind, the unsatisfactoriness began and stopped." See *SH*, 18–19, for his explanations.

6. "Joyce and the Epiphany: The Key to the Labyrinth?" *The Sewanee Review*, 72 (January–March, 1964), 71.
7. Scholes and Litz point out that in revisions in "Eveline" and "The Boarding House," "the intent is obviously to make the language more colloquial, more appropriate to the events being narrated than to the more lofty tone of the narrative persona, 'Stephen Daedalus'" (Robert Scholes and A. Walton Litz, *Dubliners, Text, Criticism and Notes* [New York: Viking Press, 1969], p. 241).
8. "The Realistic Fallacy," in *The Artist's Journey into the Interior, and Other Essays* (New York: Random House, 1965), pp. 96–97.
9. Cf. below, pp. 26–27.

Chapter Two

The Artist as Judge

IN HIS EARLY *Silhouettes,* Joyce's characters are represented as shadows. He robs them of their individuality and reduces them to their most general characteristics: "the burly figure of a man," "the smaller sharp-faced figure of a nagging woman" (*MBK*, 90). He also robs them of the ability to express their inwardness by any but the most exaggerated movement: "threatening with up-raised fist," "a blow," a pointed finger. The figures and their action are transformed into a broad, general meaning which the observer reads. Stephen makes a similar reduction in the theater, in the passage from *A Portrait* quoted above. *Silhouettes* reveals another characteristic present in all the examples I have cited—the detached observer is also an interpreter and judge.

This transformation of people and things into meanings is also a characteristic of the detailed, precisely observed epiphanies and the stories of *Dubliners.* Joyce intended them to illustrate a general judgment about the "spiritual paralysis" of Dublin. The word "judgment" is important. The precise details are never given for their own sake or to give an independent life to the object. They record a judgment of the observer, represent an interpretation, an interpretation that enforces his separation from the scene before him, yet holds him before that scene as if a prisoner of it. An example of this is the scene where the narrator of "The Sisters" is unable to pray before the body of the dead priest: "I pretended to pray but I could not gather my thoughts because the old wom-an's mutterings distracted me. I noticed how clumsily her skirt was

24

hooked at the back and how the heels of her cloth boots were trodden down all to one side" (*D*, 14). This passage might be taken as a paradigm for what happens in the form of *Dubliners*.

The details in this passage are not purposeless perceptions which distract the boy and prevent him from praying. The observed details represent the feeling that separates him from the life around him, the feeling of rejection and disgust.

The apparently disconnected actions Eveline observes from her window at the beginning of that story do not represent the absurd autonomous life which things have in some recent fiction; they reveal her own feeling of imprisonment and helplessness. They register the sluggishness of her own feelings and thought and at the same time her separation from life. Although the people and actions of *Dubliners* are not reduced to bare outlines, silhouettes, they are nonetheless robbed of their independent being and used as illustrations. The external world is reduced to a meaning, a judgment, and at the same time this technique insists on the separateness of that world from the observer.

This tendency holds true not only for the observing Stephen and the first-person narrator of "The Sisters," who are properly characters within a fiction. It also holds for that hidden narrator of the later stories. An example of this is the following description from "Ivy Day in the Committee Room," the most apparently "objective" of the stories:

> A person resembling a poor clergyman or a poor actor appeared in the doorway. His black clothes were tightly buttoned on his short body and it was impossible to say whether he wore a clergyman's collar or a layman's, because the collar of his shabby frock-coat, the uncovered buttons of which reflected the candlelight, was turned up about his neck. He wore a round hat of hard black felt. His face, shining with raindrops, had the appearance of damp yellow cheese save where two rosy spots indicated the cheekbones. He opened his long mouth suddenly to express disappointment and at the same time opened wide his very bright blue eyes to express pleasure and surprise. (*D*, 125)

The reader learns on the next page that the person is a corrupt priest. The uncertainty in the first sentence of the description, however, suggests an observer who is cut off from the scene, trying to read it from the outside. Even this uncertainty about the man's role is an ironic judgment about a shady priest involved with a political boss in some dark way. In the context of this involvement the fact that he looks like an actor takes on moral weight. The guess that he might be an actor, along with the description of his exaggerated facial reactions at the end of the paragraph, insinuates his insincerity and suggests a habit of attempting to ingratiate himself with other people. The uncertain description of his clothes, which suggests shabby disguise, further implies the ambiguity of his position. The comparison of his face to damp cheese expresses the disgust of the observer. The narrator's choice of external details in this description represents an implicit judgment that prevents the reader from sympathizing with the character. But even without such an implied moral judgment, the externality of the description would have the same effect. The reader senses the narrator's distance from the character, his lack of involvement or participation in the character's experience.

The observer's separation from the world is already a judgment of that world, for it expresses the observer's feeling of intellectual or spiritual superiority. This aspect of the narrator was a characteristic of the young Joyce. It was recorded by his brother Stanislaus in his diary: "He has, above all, a proud, wilful, vicious selfishness, out of which by times now he writes a poem or epiphany" (*DD*, 14). The apparent effacement of the self of the artist before an external reality results in the assertion of the self in the most arrogant pose of all, that of judge. The stories of *Dubliners* are in some ways like pieces of evidence in support of a general indictment. One passage in *Stephen Hero* describing Stephen's "outward self-control" as an aid to "his real indictment" reveals the way indignation can be covered by an apparent passivity: "the episode of religious fervour which was fast becoming a memory had resulted in a certain outward self-control which was now found to be useful. . . . His reluctance to debate scandal, to seem impolitely curious of others, aided him in his real indictment and was not without a satisfactory flavour of the heroic" (*SH*, 29).

The rather awkward characterization of Stephen Daedalus as an "organ of sensitiveness and intellectiveness" (*SH*, 168) indicates just the sort of self-effacement that characterizes the observing narrator of *Dubliners*. Yet the full passage from which the phrase just quoted is taken reveals the ultimate arrogance behind such a depersonalization: "No young man, specialised by fate or her stepsister chance for an organ of sensitiveness and intellectiveness, can contemplate the network of falsities and trivialities which make up the funeral of a dead burgher without extreme disgust" (*SH*, 168). Such a "specialisation" into an organ of observation seems a mantle of destiny, a high election, and at the same time it is also destined that the sensitive organ shall judge the concerns of lower beings—"the network of falsities and trivialities which make up the funeral of a dead burgher" (this is the funeral of Stephen's sister). The effacement of ego implied in the narrative mode of *Dubliners* and in this phrase—"an organ of sensitiveness and intellectiveness"—masks, and not very well, an act of great egoism. The corollary of the notion of the artist as god is the notion of the artist as divine judge.

This conception of the artist is related to the idea of vision from a great height and to Joyce's youthful enthusiasm for Ibsen, who, he has Stephen say, "has the temper of an archangel" (*SH*, 93). Richard Ellmann has called attention to this relationship by pointing out that for both Ibsen and the young Joyce truth was conceived "as more an unmasking than a revelation" (*JJ*, 55) and that this concept of truth lay behind Joyce's approval of "the quality of aloofness in Ibsen that led him to leave his country and call himself an exile. Truth as judgment and disclosure, and exile as the artistic condition: These were to be the positive and negative poles of Joyce's own state of mind" (*JJ*, 55). The artist's withdrawal to the heights of judgment is a kind of exile. This is shown clearly in a passage from one of Ibsen's poems which Ellmann quotes as a possible source for an image in Joyce's "The Holy Office":

> Now I am steel-set: I follow the call
> To the height's clear radiance and glow.
> My lowland life is lived out: and high
> On the vidda are God and Liberty
> Whilst wretches live fumbling below.
> (*JJ*, 173)[1]

The artist withdraws from the lowlands to the heights of God and Liberty, i.e., to the vantage point of God, from which he views the "fumbling" lives of "wretches" far below him. The parallel passage in "The Holy Office" reveals the same pattern:

> So distantly I turn to view
> The shamblings of that motley crew,
> Those souls that hate the strength that mine has
> Steeled in the school of old Aquinas
> Where they have crouched and crawled and prayed
> I stand, the self-doomed, unafraid,
> Unfellowed, friendless and alone,
> Indifferent as the herring-bone where
> I flash my antlers on the air.
>   (*CW*, 152)

As Stanislaus has pointed out, Joyce admired those qualities which he desired in himself (*MBK*, 95); in his praise for Ibsen he emphasizes the artist's godlike or angelic vantage point. Here is the way Joyce describes that role of the artist in his essay "Ibsen's New Drama": "He sees . . . [life] steadily and whole, as from a great height, with perfect vision and an angelic dispassionateness, with the sight of one who may look on the sun with open eyes" (*CW*, 65). Behind the conception of the artist as judge is an angelism that views the concerns of life as no more meaningful than the activities of insects. Certain characters in Joyce's fiction provide examples of this angelism. Mr. Duffy, Gabriel Conroy, and Stephen Daedalus are obvious choices, but it is also the position of the narrator of *Dubliners*.

An exaggerated version is the boy-narrator of "Araby" although it is love that separates him from the world. When his imagination is captured by spiritual desire, when "the syllables of the word *Araby* were called to me through the silence in which my soul luxuriated and cast an Eastern enchantment over me"(*D*, 32), like the speaker of Ibsen's poem he follows "the call / To the height's clear radiance and glow." His "lowland life is lived out." In his own words: "I had hardly any patience with the serious work of life which, now that it stood between me and my desire, seemed to be child's play, ugly monotonous child's play" (*D*, 32). From the heights, life seems insignificant and futile to the artist-judge. Actual life serves mainly as an irritant, a distraction that seems to keep him from spiritual fulfillment. By the same token his spiritual stance, requiring a distance from life, precludes the possibility of the participation necessary for a meaningful experience.

ᴗIn "Araby" the distance is expressed by an image of height: "I sat staring at the clock for some time and, when its ticking began to irritate me, I left the room. I mounted the staircase and gained the upper part of the house. The high cold empty gloomy rooms liberated me and I went from room to room singing. From the front window I saw my companions playing below in the street. Their cries reached me weakened and indistinct" (D, 33). At the beginning of this passage the boy is still in the normal world where the fulfillment of his desires hangs on something as mundane as having to wait for his uncle to return home with the money for the bazaar. It is a world in which dependence on something apparently external seems an obstacle to the spirit. It is the world of the clock whose "ticking began to irritate me." The boy seeks to escape, and isolation in "the high cold empty gloomy rooms" seems to offer that desired liberation. His everyday world is far below him, "weakened and indistinct."

This apparent liberation from life allows the boy only a temporary satisfaction: "I may have stood there for an hour, seeing nothing but the brown-clad figure cast by my imagination" (D, 33). In the end he must descend to seek satisfaction in the real world, to experience the frustration of his desire. Like Stephen Dedalus, he wants "to meet in the real world the unsubstantial image which his soul so constantly beheld" (AP, 65). Stephen, in this passage, is also separated from other children by his sense of superiority: "The noise of children at play annoyed him and their silly voices made him feel, even more keenly than he had felt at Clongowes, that he was different from others. He did not want to play" (AP, 64–65).

Spiritual ascent provides the distance with which the artist-judge observes "normal life." The artist, who possesses a superior spirit, withdraws himself from the world in order to judge it impersonally—in order to picture its truth which is not his truth. Yet the act of judgment by a single stroke both enforces the with-

drawal and assures the artist's superiority. It might as easily be said
that the artist judges in order to hold himself separate from and
superior to the rest of the world. The ambivalence of this position
is revealed in the anger that initiates it or at least accompanies it.
I cited earlier a passage from *A Portrait* where Stephen is pictured
as a silent observer in a series of epiphanies. The sequence begins
with a reference to this anger: "He was angry with himself for being young and the prey of restless foolish impulses, angry also with
the change of fortune which was reshaping the world about him
into a vision of squalor and insincerity. Yet his anger lent nothing
to the vision. He chronicled with patience what he saw, detaching himself from it and testing its mortifying flavour in secret"
(*AP*, 67). This passage describes precisely the "objective" point of
view of *Dubliners* and its secret motivation. It needs to be placed
alongside the passage from Stanislaus' diary quoted earlier or beside a similar notation in the diary that "Jim is beginning his novel
[*Stephen Hero*], as he usually begins things, half in anger"
(quoted in *JJ*, 152). It is further illuminated by a letter Joyce wrote
his brother in the summer of 1905, while he was writing his *Dubliners* stories: "Give me for Christ's sake a pen and an ink-bottle
and some peace of mind, and then by the crucified Jaysus, if I
don't sharpen that little pen and dip it into fermented ink and
write tiny little sentences about the people who betrayed me, send
me to hell" (*Letters*, II, 110). It is more than "people" who betray
the romantic and turn him into the realist—it is the betrayal by
imprisonment in the flesh, a betrayal such as Stephen experiences
in *A Portrait*, a "change of fortune which was reshaping the world
about him into a vision of squalor and insincerity." And although
the anger seems to lend nothing to the vision, although "he chronicled with patience what he saw, detaching himself from it," it is
the secret relish for the "mortifying flavour" of the vision that
points to its source.

Joyce made the same point in his 1912 Trieste lecture on Defoe.
Contrasting Defoe's writings with what he called "modern realism," he used terms he had used to describe his own work in *Dubliners*: "The very intensity, the very refinement of French realism
betray its spiritual origins. But you will search in vain in the
works of Defoe for that wrathful ardor of corruption which illu-

mines with pestiferous phosphorescence the sad pages of Huysmans. You will search in vain . . . for that studied ardor of indignation and protest which lacerates and caresses."[2]

Just as the objectivity masked a personal need, the passivity of the observer masks an act of aggression: "Every morning . . , he got down off the tram at Amiens St. Station instead of going on to the Pillar because he wished to partake in the morning life of the city. This morning walk was pleasant for him and there was no face that passed him on its way to its commercial prison but he strove *to pierce* to the motive centre of its ugliness" (*SH*, 30; my italics). A few pages later the aggressive image is repeated: Stephen "strove *to pierce* to the significant heart of everything" (*SH*, 33; my italics). Piercing to the heart, to "the motive centre" of the ugliness of every face that passes before him, in order to "betray the soul of hemiplegia or paralysis which many call a city" is certainly a far cry from passivity and impartiality. It suggests an active aggression toward the object, which is the corollary of the concept of art of a Flaubert or a Joyce in which style, as the total transformation of the object, is everything. It is also strongly reminiscent of the description of Joyce his brother records in his diary: "Jim has a wolf-like intellect, neither massive nor very strong, but lean and ravenous, tearing the heart out of his subject" (*DD*, 15).

This aggression is implicit in the term Stephen uses for the vision or spirit he feels appropriate for modern times, a term that could easily be applied to *Dubliners*. Stephen's word is "vivisective" (*SH*, 186), and it denotes the careful, minute, scientifically objective examination of life that is the analytic method of *Dubliners*. It also suggests the aggressive cutting up of a living thing in order to see how it is put together, in order to understand what is wrong with it, a diagnostic technique that accepts the death of the patient as merely an innocent complement. "Vivisective" is an appropriate adjective for an intellect, "lean and ravenous," that tears the heart out of its subject. This is not to say, of course, that Joyce's "vivisection" can't be very funny, as for example in "Grace." The thrust of Joyce's wit is satiric, however, rather than comic.

The deadly irony that permeates the narrative of the stories in *Dubliners* clearly stems from this same hatred of reality and the feeling of spiritual superiority which is the ground of that hatred. This irony, prominent in the passages I have quoted from *Dubliners*, is almost the governing principle in the form of the stories and, as a traditional "distancing" technique, is dualistic in nature. It is difficult to give serious weight to the elaborate interpretations of Maria in "Clay" as either a witch or the Virgin Mary,[3] for example, if one pays attention to the ruthless irony in the treatment of her. It is an irony that diminishes and ridicules its object:

> Maria was a very, very small person indeed but she had a very long nose and a very long chin. She talked a little through her nose, always soothingly: "Yes, my dear," and "No, my dear." (*D*, 99)

> There was one thing she didn't like and that was the tracts on the walks; but the matron was such a nice person to deal with, so genteel. (*D*, 100)

> And Maria laughed again till the tip of her nose nearly met the tip of her chin and till her minute body nearly shook itself asunder because she knew that Mooney meant well though, of course, she had the notions of a common woman. (*D*, 101)

> But wasn't Maria glad when the women had finished their tea and the cook and the dummy had begun to clear away the tea-things! (*D*, 101)

> She looked with quaint affection at the diminutive body which she had so often adorned. In spite of its years she found it a very tidy little body. (*D*, 101)

The repetitiveness, the frequent references to her small size, the mocking of the thought patterns of this pathetic little creature, who however pathetic is still a snob, constitute an irony of ridicule. The deepening pathos of the story does little to counter the distance from her that ridicule represents. In fact, the pathos actually extends that distance. The reader is made aware, through the narrator, of the hopelessness of her condition, but the separation between this knowledge and her ignorance of it is complete. Her blindfolding, near the end of the story, which cuts her off from an awareness of what she has touched and its relevance to her, is parallel to her figurative blindness to the truth of her life as the narrator reveals it. The children's game is a parody of the chance and circumstance, the negation of choice, which determines this woman's life, as it determines every other life in the book. The story is almost as much of a joke at her expense as the clay the children put in the saucer. The condescension with which she is treated by almost everyone matches the narrator's condescension and his ridiculing irony.[4]

If, as I believe, every narrative form proposes a certain relationship with the reader as well as constructing a relationship between the author and his world, nothing is so revealing of the relationship proposed here as this irony. In one of the many scenes in *Stephen Hero* which show Stephen making a fool of someone without his knowing it, Stephen has a sudden "longing for Cranly's presence" (*SH*, 157). Behind this "longing" of course lies the secret contradiction in Stephen's romanticism: it is not enough for Stephen merely to be alone, to be set off from the rest; he must be seen alone. This necessity accounts for the series of friends he takes into his confidence, one by one. They serve to provide reflectors for his brilliance, to interpret him for the rest of the world and carry forth his legend, and finally to "betray" him, thus emphasizing his solitude. In this particular scene there is no one to appreciate his straight-faced teasing of the dull-witted Father Healy, no one to grasp his ironies. Stephen's spiritual and intellectual superiority is incomplete without an audience. Hence, the relationship proposed by the ironic narrator of *Dubliners*. The reader is the "Cranly" in this situation. It is not enough for him to understand the pathos and sometimes bathos of the people toward whom the irony is directed. The reader is also meant to applaud the perspicacity of the narrator and affirm his difference from the world he presents.

For the narrator, irony is a means of preserving distance from the world.[5] It is a mark of the heights from which the artist views the fumbling life of the wretches on the lowlands. It is based on the dualistic assumption of the separation between pure mind or spirit and a tainted matter. There is the same division between mind or spirit and matter in each of the stories—and in each case it is a mind or spirit imprisoned by matter rather than rising above it.

This division for the narrator is already a kind of exile, which is first and foremost a spiritual condition. Just as one does not have to remain in Dublin to remain a Dubliner, as the later Joyce realized, neither does one have to leave Dublin to be exiled from it. When Stephen Dedalus leaves Dublin he is only acting out a condition he has lived spiritually all along. But it is an exile, in this sense, that will never be complete—Stephen will return. Joyce the artist will never be able to leave this Dublin behind. The book itself is a denial of the narrator's attempt to escape to spiritual heights. He is caught between two worlds, spirit and matter, and unable to live wholly in either. Here is the meaning of that passage in "The Sisters" where the narrator is unable to pray because of his fascination with the shabby clothes of the old woman.

The narrator's pretense to a spiritually aloof position is, in a sense, contradicted by his concern with the lives of those below. As a sign of the impossiblity of leaving the world behind, *Dubliners*, with all its hatred and disdain of reality, is already an attempt to get back into contact with that reality. Stephen Dedalus in *A Portrait*, realizing "that all around him life was about to awaken in common noises, hoarse voices, sleepy prayers" (*AP*, 221), shows the importance of this direction back toward the world in *Dubliners* by his opposite reaction: "Shrinking from that life he turned towards the wall, making a cowl of the blanket and staring at the great overblown scarlet flowers of the tattered wallpaper. He tried to warm his perishing joy in their scarlet glow, imagining a roseway from where he lay upwards to heaven all strewn with scarlet flowers" (*AP*, 221–22).

However great the distance between the narrator and the world he pictures, however much that picture is meant to assure the superiority of the narrator, *Dubliners* is the beginning of a recognition that there is no "roseway . . . upwards to heaven." It represents a turning back toward a world of "common noises"—though until "The Dead" it falls short of coming to terms with that world. This recognition will be discussed more fully later, but it must be kept in mind here as an important part of the "meaning" of the form of these stories. Just as almost every story in *Dubliners* shows a character who wishes to escape his condition but is unable to, the very existence of the book itself reveals a similar recognition of the inescapable on the part of its author. The hatred of reality in "the scrupulous meanness" of the manner of narration can be seen as expression of frustration stemming from the very strength of that recognition.

This demonstrates that narrative form or point of view is much more than a free choice, on a purely technical level, of a way to tell a story. It is even more than a way of "looking at" the world which colors and structures that world presented in the form. It is ultimately a way of living the world; form is the structure of an experience in the most active sense of that word. It not only represents a certain relationship to the world, it creates that relationship. In *Stephen Hero* a literary model provides Stephen a way of turning around and facing the world of actuality, an act of which *Dubliners* is the product:

> It must be said simply and at once that at this time Stephen suffered the most enduring influence of his life. The spectacle of the world which his intelligence presented to him with every sordid and deceptive detail set side by side with the spectacle of the world which the monster in him, now grown to a reasonably heroic stage, presented also had often filled him with such sudden despair as could be assuaged only by melancholy versing. He had all but decided to consider the two worlds as aliens one to another—however disguised or expressed the most utter of pessimisms—when he encountered through the medium of hardly procured translations the spirit of Henrik Ibsen. (*SH*, 40)

The dualistic attitude of the narrator of *Dubliners* is precisely the sort of possibility Stephen finds in "the spirit of Henrik Ibsen," who was able to see life "steadily and whole, as from a great height, with perfect vision and an angelic dispassionateness" (*CW*, 65). Caught halfway between spirit and matter, the young poet, like the narrator of *Dubliners*, stops just short of considering the two worlds "aliens one to another," but is unable to synthesize them. If Stephen and the narrator are unable to escape the world completely, one alternative is to withdraw into the self. Stephen's "melancholy versing" is like that of the Irish poet James Clarence

Mangan, whom, Joyce said, "sufferings drove . . . to become a hermit, and in fact he lived the greater part of his life almost in a dream, in that sanctuary of the mind where for many centuries the sad and the wise have elected to be. When a friend remarked to him that the tale . . . [of his childhood] was wildly exaggerated and partly false, Mangan answered, 'Maybe I dreamed it.' The world has evidently become somewhat unreal for him, and not very significant" (CW, 181). Like Mangan's sufferings, which "had cast him inwards" (CW, 76), Stephen's encounter with the world "had driven him from breathless flights of zeal shamefully inwards" (SH, 29).

In "A Painful Case" Mr. Duffy's disdain is a stronger version of the withdrawal inwards. He refuses to write at all: "She asked him why he did not write out his thoughts. For what, he asked her, with careful scorn. To compete with phrasemongers, incapable of thinking consecutively for sixty seconds? To submit himself to the criticisms of an obtuse middle class which entrusted its morality to policemen and its fine arts to impresarios?" (D, 111). If the narrator of Dubliners could realize his anger completely, his contempt for the world, he would not have to write the book. Compared with Mr. Duffy's refusal, Dubliners is clearly a movement toward relationship.

What Stephen finds useful in his discovery of Ibsen is more than a purely literary model, it is a spiritual attitude: "But it was not only this excellence which captivated him: it was not that which he greeted gladly with an entire joyful spiritual salutation. It was the very spirit of Ibsen himself that was discerned moving behind the impersonal manner of the artist: Ibsen with his profound self-approval, Ibsen with his haughty, disillusioned courage, Ibsen with his minute and wilful energy" (SH, 41).

Joyce's phrases in this passage describe exactly the narrator of Dubliners. The narrator's assumption of spiritual superiority is certainly a "profound self-approval"; the narrative manner of Dubliners might even be seen as an attempt to protect that self-approval. The exposure of the emptiness of ordinary life in these stories could indicate a "haughty, disillusioned courage." "Minute and wilful energy" is an appropriate way of describing the vivisective realism of the book. Joyce will later become aware of the egoism of this position. That awareness is partially revealed by a change of wording in this passage pencilled in the margin of the MS of *Stephen Hero* at a later date (*SH*, 41n). "His profound self-approval" is changed to "a mind of sincere and boylike bravery." "Haughty, disillusioned courage" becomes "disillusioned *pride*." Joyce's recognition of the "pride" in the manner of *Dubliners* and his shedding of the "illusion" that supported it make possible his change of attitude toward Stephen in *A Portrait* and *Ulysses*.

The pride that falls is already foreshadowed in the stories of *Dubliners*. Even a character as ineffectual as Little Chandler adopts momentarily a godlike view of his world and enjoys a brief sense of spiritual superiority:

> For the first time in his life he felt himself superior to the people he passed. For the first time his soul revolted against the dull inelegance of Capel Street. There was no doubt about it: if you wanted to succeed you had to go away. You could do nothing in Dublin. As he crossed Grattan Bridge he looked down the river towards the lower quays and pitied the poor stunted horses. They seemed to him a band of traps, huddled together along the river-banks, their old coats covered with dust and soot, stupefied by the panorama of sunset and waiting for the first chill of night to bid them arise, shake themselves and begone. He wondered whether he could write a poem to express his ideas. (*D*, 73)

Little Chandler's "poetic" impulse is soon smothered in the domestic prison which is as much chosen as a protection from freedom as it is encountered as an obstacle. This fact allows the narrator a feeling of superiority toward a character that might be seen as resembling him. So also does the fact that Little Chandler's brief feeling of superiority leads him to just such a notion of "melancholy versing" as the one that the narrator has forsworn in the act of writing *Dubliners*. Joyce and Stephen do leave the country, but Little Chandler is unable to get away. Still, Little Chandler's distant view of "life" is almost a parody of the narrator's:

> He turned often from his tiresome writing to gaze out of the office window. The glow of a late autumn sunset covered the grass plots and walks. It cast a shower of kindly golden dust on the un-

tidy nurses and decrepit old men who drowsed on the benches;
it flickered upon all the moving figures—on the children who ran
screaming along the gravel paths and on everyone who passed
through the gardens. He watched the scene and thought of life;
and (as always happened when he thought of life) he became
sad. A gentle melancholy took possession of him. He found how
useless it was to struggle against fortune, this being the burden
of wisdom which the ages had bequeathed to him. (*D*, 71)

This romantic glow which Little Chandler's melancholy imagination casts over his landscape—a gibe at the "Celtic Twilight"
group—is no more incomplete and unreal than the bright glare
of day in which the narrator claims to see his world. Both views
end as visions of futility. Stephen defines the "romantic" attitudes
as "an insecure, unsatisfied, impatient temper which sees no fit
abode here for its ideals" (*SH*, 78). This definition is as true of the
"realism" of the narrator as it is of Little Chandler's "Celtic" melancholy. If *Dubliners* is in some ways, in stories like "Araby," "A
Little Cloud," and "A Painful Case," a criticism of Joyce's earlier
romanticism, it represents that romanticism merely turned inside
out.

NOTES

1. Professor Ellmann is quoting M. C. Bradbrook's translation of
   Ibsen's "On the Vidda."
2. *Daniel Defoe*, ed. and trans. Joseph Prescott, *Buffalo Studies*, 1
   (December, 1964).
   Erich Heller has said that "somewhere in [the] heart" of the
   apparently objective realistic literature of the nineteenth century
   "quivers the hatred of reality and the lust for conquest." He points
   out that the attempt to give a faithful picture of social reality was
   nothing new to literature. What was new was the particular passion behind the attempt: "It is the passion of understanding, the
   desire for rational appropriation, the driving force toward the ex-
   propriation of the mystery. . . . For the 'realistic' sense of reality
   which possessed so many minds in the nineteenth century was
   such that it lured them towards the rational conquest of the human
   world only in order to prove to them its absolute meaninglessness"
   ("The Realistic Fallacy," in *The Artist's Journey into the Interior*,

and Other Essays [New York: Random House, 1965], pp. 95–96). This passion in the early Joyce already presupposes that meaninglessness in its indictment of the "squalor and insincerity" of the world.

3. See the discussion of "Clay" in Marvin Magalaner and Richard Kain, *Joyce: The Man, the Work, the Reputation* (New York: Collier Books, 1962), pp. 96–100, and also Richard Carpenter and Daniel Leary, "The Witch Maria," *The James Joyce Review*, 3 (1959), 3–7.

4. Similarly, Frank O'Connor, in commenting on the scene in "Grace" where the assembled Dubliners make silly pronouncements about church history, has pointed out that "Joyce, the ecclesiastical scholar, the all-but-Jesuit, is in a position to sneer at them all. Gorky, Leskov, or Chekov would not have sneered. Joyce's submerged population is no longer being submerged by circumstances but by Joyce's own irony" (*The Lonely Voice: A Study of the Short Story* [Cleveland: World Publishing Company, 1963], p. 123).

5. In a remarkable essay on Gustave Flaubert, Henry James observes that Flaubert's irony in works like *Bouvard et Pécuchet* and *L'Education sentimental* served as just as much of an escape from life for the writer as the more exotic subjects of books like *Salammbo*. What were both escapes, asked James, "but a confession of supreme impatience with the actual and the near"? James's questioning of the adequacy of Flaubert's irony as a complete vision of life might also be applied to the Joyce of *Dubliners*:

> And we inevitably ask ourselves whether, eschewing the policy of flight, he might not after all have fought out his case a little more on the spot. Might he not have addressed himself to the human still otherwise than in *L'Education* and in *Bouvard*? When one thinks of the view of the life of his country, of the vast French community and its constituent creatures, offered in these productions, one declines to believe it could make up the *whole* vision of a man of his quality. Or when all was said and done was he absolutely and exclusively condemned to irony? ("Gustave Flaubert," in *The Future of the Novel: Essays on the Art of Fiction*, ed. Leon Edel [New York: Vintage Books, 1956], p. 15)

James's case is probably overstated, as mine may be, for the sake of argument.

In fact, Joyce began to ask these same questions of himself before he had finished writing the series. One example is the letter to

Stanislaus in which Joyce confessed that he might have been "unnecessarily harsh. I have reproduced (in *Dubliners* at least) none of the attraction of the city" (*Letters*, II, 166). The picture of life in the *Dubliners* stories did not "make up the *whole* vision of a man of his quality." The fact that he "addressed himself still otherwise" in "The Dead" and after underlies the relevance of James's questioning. Here, however, irony is another manifestation of the division between the narrator and his world.

Chapter Three

The Artist as Mediator

THE NARRATOR'S RELATIONSHIP to his world, implicit in the form of *Dubliners*, is reflected in the various relationships between the characters and their world within those stories. Each of the characters experiences a world from which he is excluded, either by his own choice or by the choice of others or by circumstances. The first-person narrator of the first three stories, Mr. Duffy, and Gabriel Conroy are excluded by their feelings of superiority. Others, like Eveline or Maria, Little Chandler or Jimmy Doyle, Lenehan or Mr. Farrington, are excluded by circumstances or by their feelings of inferiority. At the same time, these people cannot escape the world from which they are excluded or exclude themselves. It is as if each person were trapped on the rim of a circle. He cannot get inside it and he cannot leave it altogether. He seems doomed, like Ireland, to remain on the edge of life. The narrator, as I have attempted to show, straddles the same line.

This predicament constitutes the structure of the stories on every level. It gives meaning to the most pervasive theme, the "exotic Oriental motif,"[1] which for Brewster Ghiselin and other critics provides the basic symbolic structure of the book.[2] The Oriental motif is that constant direction of the Dubliners toward an imaginary place which seems to offer relief from the spiritual impoverishment of their everyday lives. The stale prison of actuality and the exotic other place of the spirit are the broken halves of the divided world of both the characters and the narrator.

41

Ghiselin, pointing out the traditional religious meaning of the East, interprets this motif as revealing the Dubliners' "need for re-orientation of the soul" (p. 197). One must affirm the richly religious suggestiveness of the East as a motif in these stories and Ghiselin's contributions to an understanding of it. Ghiselin's interpretation is, however, misleading. He says, for example, that in "The Sisters," the boy's dream of a journey "to a churchlike place in the East, where there are 'long curtains and a swinging lamp of antique fashion,' define[s] the need of Dubliners to seek out for themselves the spiritual life that is no longer available in Ireland" (p. 197). By his allegorizing of Eastern movement in *Dubliners* as a real journey of the soul toward God, Ghiselin fails to note the distinction between realms in the book. His interpretation suggests that the soul should be able to find its true home, but the essence of the motif in the stories is the impossibility of a desired transcendence. He ignores the meaning of the exoticism of the motif.

Commenting on the ending of "Araby," Ghiselin says that "the soul's energy has carried it across water but not to the sea, far eastward but to a secular goal, not to its true orient" (p. 199; also p. 85). Again, Ghiselin's idea is that the boy might have found spiritual fulfillment in some other real place or in himself. But the point of the story is the impossibility of ever mating inner dream with outer reality.

Moreover, the fact that the Dubliners call their bazaar "Araby" shows that it represents a dream of exotic escape for all of Dublin as well as for the sensitive, moony boy.[3] Sigfried Giedion has pointed out the persistence of the Oriental influence in nineteenth-century culture, not only in its art, but also in its furnishings and decor: "Mechanized man in the nineteenth century yearned for an atmosphere other than that of his own surroundings. . . . The Oriental influence must be counted as one of the many strivings for escape that darkened the emotional life of the last century and gave it a tragic note. Man was not content to live in his own skin."[4] The exotic, Oriental, motif in *Dubliners* represents just such a need to escape and the tragic split between spirit and nature.

The image of the exotic East develops through the stories into a theme that is much wider than any particular "orientation," and greater than any particular symbol. Ghiselin's emphasis on the East must be qualified by the fact that a Western direction can also be associated with the place of desire. Eveline wants to go to Buenos Aires. The boys' journey in "An Encounter" is inspired by "literature of the Wild West" (*D*, 20). Any direction can seem to provide hope for escape to the trapped spirit. The important fact is that the desired place is always imaginary and always in opposition to the here and now. The early references to an exotic East fulfill this requirement. The dream of the boy in "The Sisters," which Ghiselin claims shows the boy's "assumption of spiritual responsibility" (p. 197), is introduced by the notion of spiritual escape from the priest: "But the grey face still followed me. It murmured: and I understood that it desired to confess something. I felt *my soul receding* into *some pleasant and vicious region*" (*D*, 11; my italics). The next day he remembers having been, in his dream, in a place where he "had noticed long velvet curtains and a swinging lamp of antique fashion. I felt that I had been very far away, in some land where the customs were strange—in Persia, I thought" (*D*, 13–14). The exotic qualities of this place would seem to connect it more with *The Rubaiyat of Omar Khayyam* than with any idea of the church. The place of the dream, however, is like that "church apart" inhabited by "the monk-errants, Ahern and Michael Robartes" in Yeats's stories "The Tables of the Law" and "Adoration of the Magi," which the young Stephen (and Joyce also) was fond of quoting: "They left their thuribles wearily before their deserted altars; they live beyond the region of mortality, having chosen to fulfil the law of their being. . . . They lean pitifully towards the earth, like vapours, desirous of sin, remembering the pride of their origins, calling others to come to them" (*SH*, 178). The point about the East in the boy's dream lies in its opposition to the actual Dublin of the old woman whose skirt was clumsily hooked at the back and whose "cloth boots were trodden down all to one side" (*D*, 14).

In the same way, in "Araby" the boy-narrator attempts to escape from reality and the flesh. First his imagined love for Mangan's sister[5] provokes this attempt: "Some distant lamp or lighted window gleamed below me. I was thankful that I could see so little. All my senses seemed to desire to veil themselves and, feeling that I was about to slip from them, I pressed the palms of my hands together until they trembled, murmuring: 'O love! O love!' many times" (D, 31). Mangan's sister is responsible for the boy's interest in Araby. Her image and the magical word separate the boy from reality: "At night in my bedroom and by day in the class-room her image came between me and the page I strove to read. The syllables of the word *Araby* were called to me through the si-lence in which my soul luxuriated and cast an Eastern enchant-ment over me" (D, 32.)

This spiritual enchantment, which so lifts the boy from actuality that it turns "the serious work of life" into "child's play, ugly monotonous child's play" (D, 32), actually represents a romantic transference of a religious impulse to a woman, but its importance lies in the fact that it is a desire for escape from life, rather than "a need for spiritual re-orientation." The point of the story, the failure of the boy's quest, which is unfortunately to a real bazaar rather than to an imaginary one, is that he is caught between two realms which cannot be joined.

Beyond any simple hope for change, the hopeless desire for es-cape takes many forms in *Dubliners*, but the place of desire always derives its significance from its opposition to actuality. Its unreal quality is a mark of its difference from the here and now. The artificiality of this exoticism is the counterpart of the form of these stories, which grants a paralyzing reality to the here and now. "An Encounter," like "Araby," is also about the failure to find the imaginary place by an actual journey, only here it is the escape literature of the Wild West which prompts the journey: "But real adventures, I reflected, do not happen to people who remain at home: they must be sought abroad" (D, 21). Here again it is the idea of the other place, the some other time, which appeals and, as always, stems from an impatience or restless dissatisfaction with the present time and place. In "Eveline" there is not only "Buenos Ayres," where Eveline hopes to find fulfillment with Frank, there is also the past when Eveline and her family were together and happy, when her mother was alive and "her father was not so bad" (D, 36–37), a past introduced by a series of "used to's," on the first page of the story. And when her present life seems about to be replaced by another, then it threatens to become desirable: "now that she was about to leave it she did not find it a wholly unde-sirable life" (*D*, 38).

Significance always exists in some other place or in some other time in these stories: London for Little Chandler, the great life in Paris for Jimmy Doyle, European culture for Mr. Duffy and Gabriel Conroy. In "The Boarding House," satisfaction for Mrs. Mooney and her daughter lies in the future, in an idea of marriage. It is the past in "Ivy Day in the Committee Room," a time when Parnell was alive—"Musha, God be with them times!" says the old man. "There was some life in it then" (*D*, 122)—a time scarcely more real than the mythical past of Maria's song in "Clay": "I dreamt that I dwelt in marble halls" (*D*, 106). The narrator of *Dubliners* also participates in a nostalgia generated by the opposi-tion to the present of a more meaningful past. This opposition is apparent, for example, in the ironic titles "Two Gallants," and "Grace," both of which represent a moral comment on the seem-ingly objective narratives and imply a contrast with a time when the irony was not necessary. This nostalgia of the narrator for a more significant past permeates the stories. It is implied for exam-ple when he says that on the night of the big race, which tem-porarily unites Ireland with the "life" of the Continent, "the city wore the mask of a capital" (*D*, 46). Even more clear is this pas-sage from "A Little Cloud": "He picked his way deftly through all that minute vermin-like life and under the shadow of the gaunt spectral mansions in which the old nobility of Dublin had roystered. No memory of the past touched him, for his mind was full of a present joy" (*D*, 71–72). This memory of the past, which serves as a criticism of the present, is the narrator's and not Little Chandler's. It is significant that the first line of the first story is "There was no hope for him this time" (*D*, 9), for "this time" holds no hope for anyone, as story after story testifies.

"The Dead" provides a kind of coda to this theme, recapitu-lating every nuance of the meaning of the some other time, some other place. In this final story, the past means something different to every character, but what unites them is that it is only the past that has meaning: a past reflected even in a detail as small as the Shakespearean scenes in the pictures on the walls at the Misses Morkan's (*D*, 186). It is the past of national honor, vitality, and hospitality that Gabriel commemorates in his after-dinner speech and the European cultural past he secretly holds in opposition to it. For Miss Ivors, it is that more radical national past which she wants to recover. It also is the past when there were great tenors and Aunt Julia still had her voice. Lily, the maid, invokes another past when she says, "The men that is now is only all palaver and what they can get out of you" (D, 178). It is the past that holds Gretta's attention when Gabriel catches her in the pose he calls "Distant Music," a past when men died for love.

That title, "Distant Music," is most appropriate, for it fits precisely the nature of the exotic other-time/other-place motif that runs throughout Dubliners. It is like the music Stephen hears in A Portrait: "He heard a confused music within him as of memories and names which he was almost conscious of but could not capture even for an instant; then the music seemed to recede, to recede, to recede: and from each receding trail of nebulous music there fell always one longdrawn calling note, piercing like a star the dusk of silence. Again! Again! Again! A voice from beyond the world was calling" (AP, 167).

The distant music that so transfixes the Dubliners and the narrator is exactly this "voice from beyond the world." Its essential quality is the uncrossable distance that separates them from what is significant. The distance between what the Dubliner is and what he desires repeats the distance that separates each Dubliner from every other and the narrator from reality. The meaning of the real or imaginary place and the real or mythical past is the feeling of separation and loss, the experience of impossible distance.

The intensity of this experience, which is built into the form of Dubliners, underlines the significance of its religious imagery and symbolism. Joyce's early description of his plans for the book when he had written only one story reveals the source of the Dubliner's feeling of loss: "I am writing a series of epicleti—ten—for a paper. I have written one. I call the series Dubliners to betray the soul of that hemiplegia or paralysis which many consider a city" (Letters, I, 55). The term epicleti is Joyce's plural for epiklesis, meaning invocation, a special prayer that occurs in all Eastern liturgies and originally in Western liturgies also. In this prayer the celebrant of the Mass prays that God may send down his Holy Spirit to change the bread and wine into the body and blood of Christ.

The Eastern church believes that the transubstantiation does not take place until the *epiklesis* is said. The wording of the prayer is especially urgent, and this urgency takes on poignance in relationship to the stories of *Dubliners*. For example, this part of the *epiklesis* in the Byzantine Liturgy of St. John Chrysostom: "We beg Thee, we ask Thee, we pray Thee that Thou, sending down Thy Holy Spirit on us and on these present gifts . . . make this bread into the Precious Body of Thy Christ . . . and that which is in the chalice, the Precious Blood of Thy Christ, changing . . . them by Thy Holy Spirit."[6] As *"epicleti"* the stories are the recognition of a terrible desolation and are prayers for a transformation. The world is waiting for the sign from heaven the way Ireland waits in the ballad "Silent O Moyle," which haunts "Two Gallants," asking "When will that day-star, mildly springing, warm our isle with peace and love? / When will heaven, its sweet bell ringing, / Call my spirit to the fields above?"

The world of *Dubliners* is an unblessed sacrament, dead matter, forgotten by a distant God. The Dubliners, unable wholly to give themselves to the world of the here and now, are also unable to receive completion from a transcendent world. They are caught like the narrator of "The Sisters," unable to pray, or like Stephen of *A Portrait*, who is incapable of raising "his soul from its abject powerlessness. God and the Blessed Virgin were too far from him: God was too great and stern and the Blessed Virgin too pure and holy" (*AP*, 116). This distance between man and God cannot be crossed. This is the heresy of Stephen's essay: the soul is "without a possibility of ever approaching nearer" to its Creator (*AP*, 79).

Brewster Ghiselin has written of the pattern of imagery throughout *Dubliners* which has to do with secular substitutes for "the water of regeneration and the wine and bread of communion, the means of approach to God":

> In *Dubliners* from first to last the substitutes are prominent, the true objects are unavailable. The priest in the first story, "The Sisters," has broken a chalice, is paralyzed, and dies; he cannot

offer communion, and an empty chalice lies on his breast in death. The food and drink obtained by the boy whose friend he has been are unconsecrated: wine and crackers are offered to him solemnly, but by secular agents. Again and again throughout *Dubliners* such substitutes for the sacred elements of the altar recur, always in secular guise. (p. 83)

As Ghiselin and others have noted, it is significant that *Dubliners* begins with the death of a priest. Such a death is mentioned again at the beginning of "Araby." Ghiselin says, "Perhaps the death of God is intimated, for . . . in a stroke of wit Joyce has given him in the very first sentence of the book an aspect of God, in stating that hope for his life was abandoned at the third onset of his malady, as if his death must be threefold" (pp. 197–98). Magalaner and Kain go further in suggesting that the priest "appears to be illustrative of the, to Joyce, decaying Irish Catholic God. Being a part of the paralyzed Irish environment, the Deity of the church is also paralyzed" (p. 84). These ideas are very suggestive. It is, however, unnecessary to substitute God for Father Flynn, which would be to read the stories as allegories.[7] The priest is man's link with God. The death of the priest at the beginning of *Dubliners* suggests the loss of that link. Even before his death, however, Father Flynn has come to realize the inefficacy of the Mass, that there was nothing in the chalice. This discovery drives him mad. In a sense, the symbolism of these stories consists in the failure of the symbolic, the emptiness of the symbol.

It also would seem inadequate to say that the desolation of this world in the book is the result of the spiritual corruption of either the people or their church. This would suggest that it lay in human hands to do something about their loss. In *A Portrait*, Stephen, suffering remorse, makes this interpretation of his predicament. His prayer suggests the reason for the division between worlds:

—He once had meant to come on earth in heavenly glory but we sinned: and then He could not safely visit us but with a shrouded majesty and a bedimmed radiance for He was God. So He came Himself in weakness not in power and He sent thee, a creature in His stead, with a creature's comeliness and lustre suited to our state. And now thy very face and form, dear mother, speak to us of the Eternal; not like earthly beauty, dangerous to look upon, but like the morning star which is thy emblem, bright and musical, breathing purity, telling of heaven and infusing peace. O harbinger of day! O light of the pilgrim! Lead us still as thou hast led. In the dark night, across the bleak wilderness guide us on to our Lord Jesus, guide us home. (*AP*, 138–39)

After Stephen has confessed, been absolved, received communion, however, his problem remains: "The clear certitude of his own immunity [from temptation] grew dim and to it succeeded a vague fear that his soul had really fallen unawares. It was with difficulty that he won back his old consciousness of his state of grace by telling himself that he had prayed to God at every temptation and that the grace which he had prayed for must have been given to him inasmuch as God was obliged to give it" (*AP*, 153). Stephen can only reason that he is in grace. It is an attempt to force his own feeling and a blasphemous attempt to oblige God. But he cannot force a union. The distance is too great and there is no bridge over it for him.

In "Araby" the boy moves into the dead priest's house and takes up his belongings—in other words, the priest is replaced by something else. Father Flynn, in "The Sisters," dies after paralysis and years of inactivity. The power of the man is replaced by the lace-curtain respectability of the two sisters with their biscuits and sherry. There is no longer any sense of the "awful power" of the priest "to make the great God of Heaven come down upon the altar and take the form of bread and wine" (*AP*, 158). The priests' ability to act as mediators between man and God is a thing of the past. Father Flynn's instruction of the boy is placed on the same level with teaching him "to pronounce Latin properly" and telling him "stories about the catacombs and about Napoleon Bonaparte" (*D*, 13). The "duties of the priest towards the Eucharist" seem to the boy "so grave . . . that I wondered how anybody had ever found in himself the courage to undertake them" (*D*, 13). The holy books of the church fathers which elucidate "all these intricate questions" are "thick as the *Post Office Directory* and as closely printed as the law notices in the newspaper" (*D*, 13) and apparently as irrelevant to the boy's life.

The whole lore of the church has the air of the vestige of some ancient practice told by a shabby old man to a young boy, or of rites so difficult as to be impossible. Even the Mass is placed into this context and robbed of its meaning. The old priest guides the boy through the responses in an empty recital of a real service: "Sometimes he used to put me through the responses of the Mass which he had made me learn by heart; and, as I pattered, he used to smile pensively and nod his head, now and then pushing huge pinches of snuff up each nostril alternately. When he smiled he used to uncover his big discolored teeth and let his tongue lie upon his lower lip—a habit which had made me feel uneasy in the beginning of our acquaintance before I knew him well" (D, 13). In this religious book, this passage is the only direct representation of a church service except for Father Purdon's sermon, praising the "worshippers of Mammon," during the businessmen's retreat in "Grace."

Throughout the book, the sacred has been secularized. There is no sense of anything existing outside human life but a great nothingness and nothing in that life but an emptiness. Father Flynn becomes unbalanced after dropping and breaking a chalice, but the significant thing is the fact that the chalice contained "nothing" (D, 17). It is not the sin of his breaking the chalice that causes his madness—it might be the realization of the meaninglessness of the act. Perhaps it is his realization of his own inefficacy as mediator, the inefficacy of the Mass, of prayer, of confession, that causes him to sit alone in the dark in an empty confession box and laugh madly to himself. There is no one, nothing, there. Because the distance between man and God is insurmountable, there is no longer anything for the priest to do. The corruption of the world, apparent throughout Dubliners, is not the cause of God's neglect but rather the result. There is no longer any hope for regeneration. The some other place/some other time that transfixes the Dubliners is the vague hope of filling the emptiness they experience.

What about the form of Dubliners and its realism? On the one hand is the idea of a creator-god who apparently leaves his world to its own unsatisfactory resources, and, on the other, the concept of an impersonal artist-god who withdraws from his creation. It seems unlikely that there is no connection between these two ideas, although it is difficult to explain the relationship. The connection is made explicit in the passage where Stephen describes the disappearing artist-god. Though his description of the where-abouts of the God of creation is indeterminate—"within or behind or beyond his handiwork"—it is the notion of withdrawal that is emphasized, the "beyond or above his handiwork, *invisible, re-fined out of existence, indifferent*, paring his fingernails" (*AP*, 215; my italics). This emphasis becomes more clear if we compare this statement with Flaubert's version, which is probably the source. Flaubert wrote that "an artist must be in his work like God in creation, invisible and all-powerful; he should be everywhere felt, but nowhere seen."[8] The most significant thing about the parallel between Flaubert's statement and Stephen's is that they are not really parallel. Flaubert's God is everywhere present in things, while Stephen's concept rules out the notion of an immanent God. Lynch's comment on Stephen's formula draws attention to this meaning. Stephen's discourse has been interrupted at just this moment by a sudden shower: "What do you mean, Lynch asked sur-lily, by prating about beauty and the imagination in this miserable *God-forsaken* island? No wonder the artist retired within or behind his handiwork after having perpetrated this country" (*AP*, 215).

The God Lynch speaks of who judges the world as unworthy and withdraws from it is not unlike the artist-judge, discussed earlier. The withdrawal of God and the withdrawal of the artist coincide. Connected with both withdrawals is the radical separation of spirit and nature, mind and matter, subject and object, the dualism which frustrates the lives of the Dubliners and is implicit in the form of the book. The withdrawal of God from the world reduces the sacrament to dead matter and robs nature of any spiritual significance. The observer-narrator of *Dubliners* draws away from the world he observes. The unmasking "realism" of the book describes a world where nothing is sacred.[9]

The gaze that separates spirit and matter is revealed in a scene in *A Portrait*. Stephen has become momentarily lost in a revery concerning the strange, seductive country woman his friend Davin had encountered:

> The last words of Davin's story sang in his memory and the figure of the woman in the story stood forth, reflected in other figures of the peasant women whom he had seen standing in the doorways at Clane as the college cars drove by, as a type of her

race and his own, a batlike soul waking to the consciousness of
itself in darkness and secrecy and loneliness and, through the
eyes and voice and gesture of a woman *without guile*, calling the
stranger to her bed.
    A hand was laid on his arm and a young voice cried:
    —Ah, gentleman, *your own girl*, sir! The first handsel today,
gentleman. Buy that lovely bunch. Will you, gentleman?
    The blue flowers which she lifted towards him and her young
blue eyes seemed to him at that instant *images of guilelessness;
and he halted till the image had vanished and he saw only her
ragged dress and damp coarse hair and hoydenish face.* (AP,
183; my italics)

Reality makes a surprising offer, coinciding with Stephen's revery. For a moment, the mental image and the actuality, inside
and outside, seem to unite. Then, as in a loss of focus, the image
breaks in two. The conscious separation Stephen makes is not simply a matter of his refusal, or inability, to idealize a shabby girl
trying to sell him flowers. The point is that revery and reality are
broken apart completely. One is left with the choice of either the
fantasy or an actuality deprived of spiritual significance. The
flower girl is as much "a type of her race and his own" as the woman Davin has told him of and that he has been dreaming about—
and as guileless. Moreover, she is a version of a traditional girl
bearing flowers. Her blue eyes and blue flowers are emblems of in-
nocence and of the Virgin, and reminiscent of the ideal blue
flower of romanticism.[10] Stephen not only refuses to bring his two
worlds into meaningful relationship, he drives further the wedge
between them. He holds his gaze until he sees "only her ragged
dress and damp coarse hair and hoydenish face."
    The narrator of *Dubliners* also is able to see only ragged dresses
and hoydenish faces. The word "disillusioned," which Stephen
applies to Ibsen, is an attitude implicit in the narration of *Dubliners.* Just as the boy's quest in "Araby" to the actual bazaar results in the loss of his illusion, so also the journey to Dublin, represented by the whole book, is meant to result in the same loss.
Disillusionment is part of what is implied in Joyce's intention of
liberating his countrymen.
    But however much this disclosure is the work of a "mind of sin-
cere and boylike bravery," however courageous his disillusion-

ment (*SH*, 41, quoted above), *Dubliners* is also a lament over the loss of a sacred sense of the world. The loss of God as both a sense or significance in things, lives, time, and as a cohesive source of unity has a universal effect in *Dubliners*. The world of this book is fragmented, a fact that has a bearing on the specific kind of unity the book has. It is not enough to point to its tight, symbolic structure, its unity of theme and motif, without underlining the fact that it is a book of separate stories, lacking the kind of surface linear unity a novel has. It is significant that the first-person narrators of the first three stories are thought to be the same boy and that boy the young Stephen Daedalus. But part of its significance stems from the fact that there is no way of proving a connection. There is no apparent continuity between the stories. There is no reference in any story to an event which has taken place in another. This lack of continuity cannot be caused by the fact that the stories were written separately, without thought of a collection. They were originally intended as a series. The idea that the narrators are the same comes merely from similarity of tone and sensibility. Life begins anew in each story and ends in the same incomplete gesture toward freedom.

This discontinuity contributes to a sense of overall apathy and frustration. Loss of spiritual significance means disorientation in both time and space. Every moment is like every other moment, without meaningful sequence because without goal. Every direction becomes like every other direction, because the Dubliners lack a center or an origin, and because all movements end in hopelessness. Because there is no hope in this time, then there are no consequences to action, no end but in death, nothingness. This is the world of *Dubliners*, before Joyce wrote "The Dead."

The loss of a sense of the significance in things is the opposite of the world in *Ulysses*, in which things have their own speech and God is a shout in the streets. Joyce's choice of the word *epicleti* to describe *Dubliners* is the first implication of a new function of the artist that will become a major motif in his work. If these stories are invocatory prayers, the person who makes the prayer, who pleads for the transformation of dead matter into meaningful world, is the priest. This role is implied in the instruction and dream of the boy in "The Sisters," and in the fact that the nar-

rator of "Araby" moves into the house of a dead priest and thinks
of himself as bearing "my chalice safely through a throng of foes"
(*D*, 31). The *epiklesis* of *Dubliners* is the recognition of a spiritual
disorder. The stories are prayers for transformation. The artist-
priest stands between two irreconcilable worlds. Joyce described
exactly this function in an early essay on Ibsen: "Here the artist
forgoes his very self and stands a mediator in awful truth before
the veiled face of God" (*CW*, 42). Later Joyce will see the artist's
role as priest differently. Instead of mediating between two
worlds, he will unite them. He will become "a priest of eternal
imagination, transmuting the daily bread of experience into the
radiant body of everliving life" (*AP*, 221). That transformation
will be one of the major themes in *Ulysses*, and perhaps the principle of its form.

NOTES

1. Magalaner and Kain's phrase, in *Joyce: The Man, the Work, the
   Reputation* (New York: Collier Books, 1962), p. 72. Further references to this book will be identified in the text.
2. See Brewster Ghiselin, "The Unity of Joyce's 'Dubliners,'" *Accent*, 16 (Spring–Summer, 1956), 75–83, 196–213, for the fullest
   discussion of this theme, esp. pp. 78–79 and the passages quoted
   below. Further citations of this article will be identified in the
   text. See also the essays by John William Carrington, Fritz Sinn,
   and J. S. Atherton in *James Joyce's Dubliners*, ed. Clive Hart
   (London: Faber, 1969).
3. Herbert Howarth, *The Irish Writers: 1830–1940* (New York: Hill
   and Wang Dramabook, 1959), passim, esp. p. 262, has shown
   the pervasiveness of Oriental themes in Joyce's Irish contempo-
   raries and predecessors.
4. *Mechanization Takes Command: A Contribution to Anonymous
   History* (New York: Oxford University Press, 1948), p. 370.
5. Herbert Howarth in *The Irish Writers* (p. 262) has called attention to the relevance of Joyce's essay about the Irish writer
   James Clarence Mangan to "Mangan's sister" and the Oriental
   motif in "Araby." (See also Magalaner and Kain, p. 89.) But
   Howarth seems to think the Orient here represents the "sensuous":
   " 'Mangan's sister' is the Orient, the East that complements the

West of his mind . . . the polar opposite of his intellect." The passage he quotes from Joyce's essay and other passages, as well as the context in "Araby" quoted below, make it clear that the Orient represents spiritual escape. Here is the passage from Joyce's paper that Howarth quotes: "East and West meet in that personality (we know how): images interweave there like soft luminous scarves and words ring like brilliant mail, and whether the song is of Ireland or of Istambol it has the same refrain, a prayer that peace may come again to her who has lost her peace, the moon-white pearl of his soul, Ameen. . . . How the East is laid under tribute for her and must bring all its treasure to her feet." In a later lecture (1907) on Mangan, Joyce repeats this passage and adds: "This figure which he adores recalls the spiritual yearnings and the imaginary loves of the Middle Ages" (*CW*, 182).

Throughout both studies, Joyce speaks of Mangan's unhappiness and suffering which "cast him inwards" (*CW*, 76) and made him consider life a dream: life for Mangan is a "malady of the spirit," a "heavy penance." His withdrawal into opium dreams and into "the lore of many lands . . . eastern tales, and the memory of curiously printed medieval books which have rapt him out of his time" (*CW*, 77) represents the same escape from the body that the Oriental motif suggests in *Dubliners*. Only now in death, Joyce said, Mangan "rests, and remembers no more this bitter vestment of the body" (*CW*, 81).

The figure of the beloved woman in Mangan's poetry Joyce aligns with Vittoria Colonna, Laura, Beatrice, and the Mona Lisa, to form an archetype encountered again in *Stephen Hero* and *A Portrait*. All these women, Joyce wrote, "embody one chivalrous idea, which is no mortal thing, bearing it bravely above the accidents of lust and faithlessness and weariness" (*CW*, 79). To this group must be added "Mangan's sister." Her image is the "chalice" in the boy's statement "I imagined that I bore my chalice safely through a throng of foes" (*D*, 31), which echoes the phrase in Joyce's essay.

6. *The Catholic Encyclopedia*, 15 vols. (New York: Robert Appleton, 1909), Vol. 5, p. 502. Another meaning of *epiklesis* is accusation; see above p. 26 and Viking Critical edition of *Dubliners*, pp. 255–56.

7. These critics must be given a great deal of credit for illuminating these stories. As Magalaner and Kain point out (p. 86), the symbolic readings are a correction of the tendency to dismiss all the

stories except "The Dead" as trivial sketches. In my quibbling with them, I certainly do not mean that symbolical interpretation of realistic fiction is necessarily a misinterpretation. Far from it. What I do want to establish is the fact that realism itself has a meaning that should not be ignored. At least part of the "symbolism" of *Dubliners* has to do with the failure or inadequacy of the symbol.

8. His letter to Mademoiselle Leroyer de Chantepie, March 13, 1857, in *The Selected Letters of Gustave Flaubert*, trans. and ed. Francis Steegmuller (New York: Farrar, Straus and Young, 1953), p. 195.

9. In 1899 Joyce wrote an essay on Munkacsy's realistic painting of Christ before Pilate, "Ecce Homo." The essay is a dramatic description of the painting, which, Joyce finds, demythologizes its subject: "The artist has chosen to make Mary a mother and John a man" (*CW*, 36). And Christ? "There is nothing divine in his look, there is nothing superhuman" (*CW*, 36). "It is literally Behold the Man. . . . It is grand, noble, tragic, but it makes the founder of Christianity no more than a great social and religious reformer, a personality, of mingled majesty and power, a protagonist of a world-drama. No objections will be lodged against it on that score by the public, whose general attitude when they advert to the subject at all, is that of the painter, only less grand and less interested" (*CW*, 37).

That Joyce interpreted the theme of the painting as "the drama of the thrice told revolt of humanity against a great teacher" (*CW*, 36) is interesting in connection with his later identification of Stephen with Christ.

10. See, for example, Novalis' novel *Henry von Ofterdingan*. Also, Joyce called Nora his blue flower several times in the letters.

II
Reunion

Chapter Four

The Artist as Hero

THE STRUCTURE OF *Dubliners* develops as an ever-increasing division between observer and observed until it reaches the ultimate division at the end of "Grace." Joyce at first planned to end the book with this story. Here is his own description of its organization: "The order of the stories is as follows. *The Sisters, An Encounter* and another story [*Araby*] which are stories of my childhood; *The Boarding House, After the Race* and *Eveline*, which are stories of adolescence; *The Clay, Counterparts* and *A Painful Case*, which are stories of mature life; *Ivy Day in the Committee Room, A Mother* and the last story of the book [*Grace*] which are stories of public life in Dublin" (*Letters*, II, 111).

On December 3, 1905, Joyce sent the manuscript of those twelve stories to a publisher, Grant Richards, who accepted it for publication on February 17, 1906, and signed a contract for it in March. Shortly after submitting the book to Richards, Joyce completed two more stories: "Two Gallants," which he sent to Richards on February 23, 1906, and "A Little Cloud," which was ready by April 23, 1906. They were to be inserted in the middle and therefore did not change the plan of the book; *Dubliners* still would have ended with "Grace." Then Joyce's troubles with Richards began and continued for several years. Until September of 1907, when "The Dead" was written, little was done to change the structure of the book. As Ellmann has noted, Joyce had begun to show some uneasiness about the nature of *Dubliners* in his letters to Stanislaus. His battle with Richards, however, "stiffened [his] sense of mission and obliterated his fears . . . that his impulsion in the stories was 'mischievous' " (*JJ*, 230) and that they might be "caricatures" of Dublin life (*Letters*, II, 99). Years later Joyce would characterize the stories as "bitter and sordid" (*Letters*, I, 70).

By the end of September, 1906, Joyce's negotiations with Richards had broken down completely and Richards refused to publish *Dubliners* (*JJ*, 239–40). At about this same time Joyce began to think of "The Dead," and it was during this time that he expressed his gravest doubts about *Dubliners* in his letters to Stanislaus (*JJ*, 239, 254; *Letters*, II, 166). "The Dead" was then begun in Trieste the following March and finished there in September of 1907. It adds a totally new element to the form of the book, bringing to the surface its divided structure and finally resolving it.

The *Stephen Hero* manuscript reveals this same structure, although critics have a habit of discussing it as if it were a much earlier work. The part that remains was written at about the same time as the main body of *Dubliners*. This is the chronology of the composition of the stories: "The Sisters," "Eveline," "After the Race," and "Clay" were written during the latter half of 1904 (*JJ*, 169, 170, 191, 196). The first version of "A Painful Case" was written either then or in early 1905, for it was rewritten and dated May 8, 1905 (*JJ*, 215). "The Boarding House," "Counterparts," "Ivy Day," "An Encounter," "A Mother," "Araby," and "Grace" were written between July and October, 1905 (*JJ*, 215). "Two Gallants," "A Little Cloud," and "The Dead" were written in early 1906 and late 1907. So the core of *Dubliners* was written during 1905.

The "Additional Manuscript Pages" at the end of the published version of *Stephen Hero* (pp. 237–53) were apparently the earliest written and preceded in Joyce's scheme the first part (presumably the end of Chapter 15). Details from the pages—Mr. Fulham and the peasant anecdote he disapproves of, for example—are discussed by Joyce in a letter to his brother on February 7, 1905 (*Letters*, II, 79). In this letter he also announces that he has finished Chapters 15 and 16 and "am now at Chap. XVII" (*Letters*, II, 81). These are the first chapters of the published version. It is clear that the chapter numbers mentioned in the letter coincide with those of the published *Stephen Hero* because Joyce also says that he is " 'working in' Hairy Jaysus at present," and Hairy Jaysus is his pet name for Francis Skeffington, the "McCann" of Chapter 17 in the published version.

Most of the remaining chapters, 17 through 24, were written between February and June of 1905 (*JJ*, 200, 215), that is, between the *Dubliners* stories composed in late 1904 and the remaining ones, written during the last half of 1905. "A Painful Case" was rewritten at the same time Joyce was working on his novel, and he probably also planned and sketched out the other stories during the spring of 1905. Chapter 25 and the fragment of Chapter 26, which end the book or in which, as Ellmann says, the book "bogged down" (*JJ*, 231), were written either shortly after the preceding ones or at the latest by July, 1906.

These dates show that the chronological connection between *Stephen Hero* and *Dubliners* is very close indeed. This connection is underscored by Joyce's decision to rewrite his novel completely and, apparently, according to the plan of *A Portrait* while he was writing "The Dead" (*JJ*, 274). I believe that this story changes the nature of *Dubliners*. My argument is that *Stephen Hero* was rejected for the same reasons that *Dubliners* was transformed. The transformation of *Stephen Hero* into *A Portrait of the Artist as a Young Man* and the resolution of *Dubliners* in "The Dead" are parallel movements, brought about by Joyce's developing awareness of their meaning.

One of the most curious things about the criticism of *Dubliners* is that the technical mastery and maturity of vision of these stories are everywhere taken for granted. Paradoxically, however, it is the immaturity of both vision and technique which is blamed for the flaws of the *Stephen Hero* fragment. In 1934, when Joyce learned that this manuscript was up for sale, he himself described it as "rubbish"[1] and later as "a schoolboy's production" (*SH*, 8). It is necessary to reconcile the simultaneous maturity and so-called immaturity in these contemporaneous works. The solution is probably to be found in investigating not the differences between the two, but rather their similarities. Many critics have pointed out that their excellences are the same—the pictorial quality, the character sketches, the dialogue. These excellences point to the common conception of the truth of the world "out there." What works in *Dubliners*, however, fails to work in *Stephen Hero*.

In *Stephen Hero* Joyce attempted not only a revelation of the truth of the world out there but also a portrait of the self that sees the truth. *Stephen Hero* is the divided world of *Dubliners*, but in *Stephen Hero* the hidden half of that world is brought into the picture. The failure of *Stephen Hero* is that the exposure of the invisible observer is not accompanied by a recognition of his true relationship to the world he perceives.

> The deadly chill of the atmosphere of the college paralysed Stephen's heart. In a stupor of powerlessness he reviewed the plague of Catholicism. He seemed to see the vermin begotten in the catacombs in an age of sickness and cruelty issuing forth upon the plains and mountains of Europe. Like the plague of locusts described in Callista they seemed to choke the rivers and fill the valleys up. They obscured the sun. Contempt of [the body]² human nature, weakness, nervous tremblings, fear of day and joy, distrust of man and life, hemiplegia of the will, beset the body burdened and disaffected in its members by its black tyrannous lice. Exultation of the mind before joyful beauty, exultation of the body in free confederate labours, every natural impulse towards health and wisdom and happiness had been corroded by the pest of these vermin. The spectacle of the world in thrall filled him with the fire of courage. He, at least, though living at the furthest remove from the centre of European culture, marooned on an island in the ocean, though inheriting a will broken by doubt and a soul the steadfastness of whose hate becomes as weak as water in siren arms, would live his own life according to what he recognized as the voice of a new humanity, active, unafraid and unashamed. (*SH*, 194)

The structure of both *Dubliners* and *Stephen Hero* centers on the idea expressed in this passage. Here is the same "spectacle of the world in thrall" that appeared in *Dubliners*. The "contempt of human nature, weakness, nervous tremblings, fear of day and joy, distrust of man and life, hemiplegia of the will" plagued the characters of that book just as they do other people in this one. Stephen's idea of other people is the world of *Dubliners*. In the final lines of this passage also is the same assumption that Stephen can detach himself from that world, stand apart and judge it, that is implicit in the narration of *Dubliners*.

In *Stephen Hero*, the narrative mode is different. The relationship between the observing character Stephen and the observing narrator must be analyzed. The third-person narration of *Stephen Hero* is a deception, at least as far as Stephen is concerned. It is really a first-person narration disguised behind the apparent distancing and objectivity of the third person. Like that habit of mind of Mr. Duffy of "A Painful Case" it is a false objectivity that affords no self-knowledge: "He had an odd autobiographical habit which led him to compose in his mind from time to time a short sentence about himself containing a subject in the third person and a predicate in the past tense" (*D*, 108). Just as the first publication of some of the stories in *Dubliners* was under the signature of Stephen Daedalus, the narrator of *Stephen Hero* is that same sensibility. In fact, according to Stanislaus, Joyce planned to give the novel the same signature: "In order further to identify himself with his hero, he announced his intention of appending to the end of the novel the signature, Stephanus Daedalus Pinxit" (*MBK*, 244). The third person of the narration is really only a thin mask meant to give the narrator the appearance of objectivity and some secrecy. As Stanislaus noted in his diary at the time, "Jim is thought to be very frank about himself but his style is such that it might be contended that he confesses in a foreign language —an easier confession than in the vulgar tongue" (quoted in *JJ*, 153).

This thin mask allows the narrator to praise Stephen extravagantly and to validate Stephen's own high estimate of himself:

> He smiled to think that these people in their hearts feared him as an infidel and he marvelled at the quality of their supposed beliefs. Father Butt talked to him a great deal and Stephen was nothing loth to make //himself the herald// of a new order. He never spoke with heat and he argued always as if he did not greatly care which way the argument went, at the same time never losing a point. The Jesuits and their flocks may have said to themselves: the //youthful seeming-independent// we know, and the

appeasable patriot we know, but what are you? They played up to him very well, //considering their disadvantages, and Stephen could not understand why they took the trouble to humour him//. (*SH*, 42)

This is followed by a brief scene in which Stephen makes a fool of the well-meaning Father Butt, as a concrete illustration, by the narrator, of Stephen's superiority. Despite the lack of any real unity to the book, almost every page of *Stephen Hero* provides examples of this extravagance which would not be allowed in a first-person narration. At the same time it is this extravagance that exposes the deception of the third-person narrator: "It was in favour of this young man that Stephen decided to break his commandment of reticence. Cranly, on his side, must have been above all the accidents of life if he had not suffered a slight commotion from such delicately insistent flattery. Stephen spoke to his impoverished ear out of the plenitude of an amassed vocabulary, and confronted the daring commonplaces of his companion's moods with a complex radiance of thought" (*SH*, 124).

This same thin deception, this distance that is no distance, accounts for most of the banalities of the narration, for they occur most often when the narrator is describing Stephen or placing him in a superior relationship to his world. Just as Stephen judges that the Jesus of the cheap print at the Daniels' exposes "his heart somewhat too obviously" (*SH*, 44), this judgment "somewhat too obviously" exposes his own sense of superiority. The use of a third-person narrator is just as obvious. It is the brave stridency of the third person that gives a Tom Swift–Rover Boys silliness to many passages:

> Neither of the youths had the least suspicion of themselves; they both looked upon life with frank curious eyes (Maurice naturally serving himself with Stephen's vision when his own was deficient) and they both felt it was possible to arrive at a sane understanding of so-called mysteries if one only had patience enough. On their way in every evening the heights of argument were traversed and the younger boy aided the elder bravely in the building of an entire science of esthetic. (*SH*, 36)

The suggestion of the ingenuousness of Stephen and Maurice at the beginning of this passage—"Neither of the youths had the least suspicion of themselves"—is meant to give a sense of distance between the narrator and them. It is a claim of objectivity, yet the rest of the passage violates the claim as the narrator gradually succumbs to the boys' own arrogant estimate of what they are engaged in. Later the narrator can say without the slightest hint of irony that "this strangely unpopular manifesto was traversed by the two brothers phrase by phrase and word by word and at last pronounced flawless at all points" (*SH*, 81). Indeed in such passages as "the poetic phenomenon is signalled in the heavens, exclaimed this heaven-ascending essayist" (*SH*, 80), passages that are parodied successfully in *Ulysses* and *Finnegans Wake*, it is the narrator himself who has little suspicion of himself ("heaven-ascending essayist" is only weakly ironic). But these banalities of style, which often are assumed to be merely the mark of a young writer, must stem from some source other than Joyce's lack of experience with the "craft" of words. *Dubliners* is clear evidence of this young writer's ability.

The source of the inadequacy of the passages dealing with Stephen must be sought instead in the suggestion of division that occurs in this description of Stephen's sensibility: "For his part he was at the difficult age, dispossessed and necessitous, sensible of all that was ignoble in such manners, who in revery, at least, had been acquainted with nobility" (*SH*, 193). The awareness of the ignoble external world, the direct experience of it, informs *Dubliners* and the portrait of Stephen's friends in *Stephen Hero*. This is a thoroughly detailed, concretely annotated picture. The other half of this divided world, however, is the vague acquaintance with nobility in revery, the dream of a subjectivity that considers itself separate from the "real" world. This revery, then, is the source of the "noble" style of the passages just quoted. I am not suggesting that there is a real other world of which the callow Stephen has inadequate experience. It is merely his division of the world into a false object and a false subject that creates this split in the style and the structure of *Stephen Hero*. Of course, *Stephen Hero* is not limited to the themes I discuss, nor is it completely without irony. It is a general tendency that I outline, and although the irony the narrator directs toward the hero is generally shallow and often self-serving, its presence indicates some awareness of the problem on Joyce's part.

Just as this "confession in a foreign language" allows Stephen as narrator to present an exaggerated estimate of himself, so too the apparently objective, third-person criticism that accompanies it is turned into self-justification. The most frequent critical epithet applied to Stephen is "egoist," yet just as often the narrator shows Stephen's egoism to be justified. For example, when Stephen visits the Daniels' home he sits on the sideline, characteristically watching the others play their games. "But," the reader is told, "whenever there was an approach to artistic matters during the process of their games Stephen with egoistic humour imagined his presence acting as a propriety" (*SH*, 43). This would seem to be criticism of Stephen's self-important habit of turning everything toward himself. The narrator, however, immediately undercuts this quite accurate criticism with a little epiphany showing that the other young people do in fact act as Stephen thinks, that "his presence" is indeed "acting as a propriety."

At another point this sort of self-justification offered as criticism becomes the occasion for a speech by the narrator that reveals the narrative process of the book. Stephen has shown his essay to his friend Madden, who disappoints him by thinking of it as poetical—"flowery" and "musical." Madden adds further insult by showing Stephen a silly poem by another friend—"Art thou real, my Ideal?"—obviously unable to tell the difference between the two works. The narrator comments that Stephen "was foolish enough to regret having yielded to the impulse for sympathy from a friend." This attempt at distancing, already weak, is thoroughly nullified by the passage that follows: "When a demand for intelligent sympathy goes unanswered [it] he is a too stern disciplinarian who blames himself for having offered a dullard an opportunity to participate in the warmer movement of a more highly organised life. So Stephen regarded his loan of manuscripts as elaborate //flag-practices with phrases//" (*SH*, 83).

Stephen's folly is apparently only in being too hard on himself, "a too stern disciplinarian." Not only has he asked for the "intelligent sympathy" which is his due from a friend, he has also offered to an inferior a great prize, the opportunity "to participate in the warmer movement of a more highly organised life." What appeared first as a criticism of Stephen becomes the most extravagant of all claims. This passage could almost be taken as a model of the whole book, for here is a more detailed suggestion of the proposed relationship with the reader mentioned earlier. Here is the same longing for an audience, but here also is the offer extended to the reader, "dullard" though he may be, to participate in a superior vision.

More than that, like Stephen's loans of manuscripts, the *Stephen Hero* narrative is "elaborate flag-practices with phrases," an attempt at breaking through the solitary prison and establishing contact with the outside world. It is a contact, however, that requires the reader's acceptance of the self-justification. The criticism of Stephen offered in the third person in this fragment always becomes a mode of self-justification, the kind of modest self-deprecation a person uses in speaking about himself. The narrator himself captures the paradoxical nature of this criticism that takes away nothing when he says, "Stephen did not in the least shrink from applying the reproach to himself but he found himself honestly unable to admit its justice" (*SH*, 126).

The same principle of doing justice to the other without admitting justice to the self lies behind the structure of *Stephen Hero*, especially in the aspect of it which is the same as the structure of *Dubliners*. The title is taken from the ballad "Turpin Hero," which relates the exploits of an eighteenth-century highwayman named Dick Turpin. Hugh Kenner has pointed out the similarity between the ballad and Joyce's novel.[3] In the various versions of the ballad, Turpin terrorizes a series of hypocritical members of the bourgeoisie, a lawyer, an exciseman, a usurer, a judge. He exposes and ridicules them and finally rids them of their money. In short, he administers justice, since they are regarded more evil than he. The lawyer, for example, Turpin "rifled of his store, / Because he knew how to lye for more."[4] At the end of the ballad, on the other hand, Turpin is caught and sentenced to hang for a trivial matter, in most versions for the "shooting of a dunghill cock"; hence he is the victim of a great injustice by society. Enemy of society, respectability, and hypocrisy, this heroic outlaw is condemned by an unjust society; Turpin is obviously a model for the romantic Stephen.

Stephen Hero is largely a series of scenes in which Stephen triumphs intellectually and morally over one after another representative of society: his friends McCann, Madden, Lynch,

Cranly, Emma, Father Butt, Father Healy, the president of the college, his brother Maurice, his father, even his mother. These scenes constitute the most amusing parts of the book. Like Stephen and Maurice, however, neither the narrator nor Stephen seems to have "the least suspicion of [himself]" (*SH*, 36; my brackets) or of his motives, for some scenes are embarrassing. Consider for example Stephen's ruthless, hypocritical treatment of Mr. Heffernan for his godfather's approval (*SH*, 246–49), or his triumph over his mother (*SH*, 132–35), a poor adversary, who provides a victory that sends Stephen "expressly to see Cranly and . . . narrate his latest conflict with orthodoxy" (*SH*, 136).

The notoriety of Stephen's interview with the college president and his triumph over the threatened censorship of his essay give him a great satisfaction: "His account of the interview went the rounds of the undergraduate classes and he was much amused to observe the startled expression of many pairs of eyes which, to judge from their open humiliated astonishment, appeared to behold in him characteristics of a moral Nelson" (*SH*, 99). Unfortunately there were no witnesses to the interview; appreciation of Stephen's triumph depends on his own account: "Stephen himself, in default of another's service, began to annotate the incident copiously, expending every suggestive phase of the interview" (*SH*, 99). This is an apt description of the narrator also, who, of course, was present at the interview, for the reader's benefit (or rather for Stephen's).

The narrator, as a substitute Cranly, a mask invented by a solitary ego, provides this service throughout the book. He is necessary for Stephen's solitary moments, obviously. Besides the kind of overt triumphs mentioned above, conversations which the narrator need only repeat, he must also reveal Stephen's more implicit triumphs, as in his boredom at the Misses Daniel's or at Father Dillon's sermon. The narrator must reveal the constant betrayal of Stephen by the insensitivity of his society, his friends, or his family. In addition, he implicitly supports Stephen in the way he characterizes Stephen's friends, in descriptions very like those in *Dubliners*:

> The teacher was a young man in spectacles with a very sick-
> looking face and a very crooked mouth. He spoke in a high-

pitched voice and with a cutting Northern accent. He never lost
an opportunity of sneering at seoninism and at those who would
not learn their native tongue. He said that Beurla was the language of commerce and Irish the speech of the soul and he had
two witticisms which always made the class laugh. One was the
"Almighty Dollar" and the other was the "Spiritual Saxon." Everyone regarded Mr Hughes as a great enthusiast and some thought
he had a great career before him as an orator. (*SH*, 59)

With this catalogue of precise details the narrator-highwayman
has set up his victim and now proceeds mercilessly to expose him
as a fraud:

> On Friday nights when there was a public meeting of the League
> he often spoke but as he did not know enough Irish he always
> excused himself at the beginning of his speech for having to speak
> to the audience in the language of the [gallant] "Spiritual Saxon."
> At the end of every speech he quoted a piece of verse. He scoffed
> very much at Trinity College and at the Irish Parliamentary Party.
> He could not regard as patriots men who had taken oaths of al-
> legiance to the Queen of England and he could not regard as a
> national university an institution which did not express the reli-
> gious convictions of the majority of the Irish people. His speeches
> were always loudly applauded and Stephen heard some of the
> audience say that they were sure he would be a great success at
> the bar. On enquiry, Stephen found that Hughes, who was the
> son of a Nationalist solicitor in Armagh, was a law-student at
> the King's Inns. (*SH*, 59–60)

Needless to say, Hughes's becoming a barrister will require the
same allegiance to the law of the Queen of England that he so
scorns (see Stephen's argument with Madden on this point, *SH*,
63). Not only are Stephen's satiric insights those of the narrator
as well, but the narrator, like Stephen, is a kind of Dick Turpin
who steals from the rich and respectable and gives, not to the
poor, but to Stephen. What is this but the structure of *Dubliners*?
Dubliners too is a series of raids on, and exposures of, the petty,
hypocritical lives of the respectable by a masked narrator who is
identical in sensibility with Stephen and the narrator of *Stephen
Hero*. In *Dubliners*, also, it is a matter of robbing the other in
support of the self, for Stephen's model is not the complete hero
he thinks he is. By robbing his victims of their wealth, however
undeserved it may be, he proves himself as materialistic as they.

The reader sees not that the respectable members of society are
no better than a highwayman, but that Stephen the highwayman
is no better than they are.

The connection between Turpin-Stephen and the high moral
claim Joyce makes for *Dubliners* in his letters becomes clearer in
the light of the statement in *Stephen Hero* that "civilisation may
be said indeed to be the creation of its outlaws" (*SH*, 178). Just as
Stephen hoped his essay would liberate his fellow students (*SH*,
49), so Joyce intended *Dubliners* to be "the first step towards the
spiritual liberation of [his] country" (*Letters*, I, 63). He hoped it
would prepare the way for a new order; he thought his giving the
Irish people "one good look at themselves in [his] nicely polished
looking-glass" would advance "the course of civilisation" (*Letters*,
I, 64). Stephen grudgingly comes to an idea of his dangerous
function in opposing society. His determination to fulfill the laws
of his own being necessarily must come into conflict with the established order, although "the attitude which was constitutional
with him was a silent self-occupied, contemptuous manner," and
although "he acknowledged to himself in honest egoism that he
could not take to heart the distress of a nation, the soul of which
was antipathetic to his own" (*SH*, 146). The social order must be
modified, for its own good:

> He wished to express his nature freely and fully for the benefit of
> a society which he would enrich and also for his own benefit, see-
> ing that it was part of his life to do so. It was not part of his life
> to undertake an extensive alteration of society but he felt the
> need to express himself such an urgent need, such a real need, that
> he was determined no conventions of a society, however plausibly
> mingling pity with its tyranny, should be allowed to stand in his
> way, and though a taste for elegance and detail unfitted him for
> the part of demagogue, [in] from his general attitude he might
> have been supposed not unjustly an ally of the collectivist poli-
> ticians. (*SH*, 146–47)

It is through this web of contradictions and qualifications that
the lonely egoist becomes another version of Christ, albeit "a disdainful Jesus" (*SH*, 178). Paradoxically, the poet-outlaw who
stands apart and judges society becomes "the intense centre of the
life of his age to which he stands in a relation than which none

can be more vital. . . . The age, though it bury itself fathoms deep
in formulas and machinery, has need of these realities which alone
give and sustain life and it must await from those chosen centres of
vivification the force to live, the security for life which can come
to it only from them. Thus the spirit of man makes a continual affirmation" (*SH*, 80).

If spiritual affirmation, "security for life," comes from art, then
the importance of simony as a theme in both *Dubliners* and *Stephen Hero* is in the relinquishing of freedom in order to attain
material security—the failure of Eveline, the cowardice of Little
Chandler. In terms of the basic dualism of the two books, simony
represents a surrender to the external world, a surrender to the
other:

> He cursed the farce of Irish Catholicism: an island [whereof]
> the inhabitants of which entrust their wills and minds to others
> that they may ensure for themselves a life of spiritual paralysis, an
> island in which all the power and riches are in the keeping of
> those whose kingdom is not of this world, an island in which
> Caesar [professes] confesses Christ and Christ confesses Caesar
> that together they may wax fat upon a starveling rabblement which
> is bidden ironically to take to itself this consolation in hardship
> "The Kingdom of God is within you." (*SH*, 146)

Stephen refuses this exchange: "I will not be frightened into
paying tribute in money or in thought" (*SH*, 141). He "voluntarily
outlaws himself" (*SH*, 148) from church and society: "He was
aware that though he was nominally in amity with the order of
society into which he had been born, he would not be able to continue so. The life of an errant seemed to him far less ignoble than
the life of one who had accepted the tyranny of the mediocre because the cost of being exceptional was too high" (*SH*, 179). Part
of the meaning of the allusions to Christ associated with Stephen
throughout the book lies in the fact that ironically it is the analogy
of "Jesus, the magnificent solitary" (*SH*, 42–43) on which this vio-
lation is based. Just as Christ triumphed over Satan's temptation,
Stephen will refuse the tempting voices of church and state (*SH*,
222, 204–9). The example of Jesus is made to support Stephen's
denial of what he considers to be the simoniacal demands of his
parents: "the narrative of the life of Jesus did not in any way im-

press him [with] as the narrative of the life of one who was subject to others" (*SH*, 111). The consequence of Stephen's battle
with society, Cranly prophesies, will be the same as Christ's (and
Dick Turpin's)—crucifixion (*SH*, 140).

Scholes and Kain have found support for Stephen's radical individualism in one of Joyce's favorite Oscar Wilde essays, "The
Soul of Man under Socialism," which he asked permission to trans-
late into Italian. In that essay such individualism is justified by
the model of Christ: "And so he who would lead a Christlike life
is he who is perfectly and absolutely himself" (quoted in *Workshop*, 280). Obviously Stephen intends such a goal. The attempt,
however, to be "perfectly and absolutely himself," besides being
Christ-like, is the error of Ibsen's Peer Gynt and, at least on the
terms set by Stephen and Peer, the attempt is doomed from the
start. To achieve absolute selfhood Stephen attempts to separate
himself from his world but, as Kenner points out, Stephen can
never be free of Dublin because he is formed on a denial of Dublin's values (p. 112).

NOTES

1. In a letter, April 7, 1934, to Harriet Shaw Weaver, quoted in John
   J. Slocum and Herbert Cahoon, *A Bibliography of James Joyce*
   (New Haven: Yale University Press, 1953), p. 136. See also *JJ*, 696.
2. For explanation of the markings in passages from *Stephen Hero*,
   see p. 22, n. 5.
3. *Dublin's Joyce* (Boston: Beacon Press Paperback, 1962), pp. 109–
   10. See *AP*, 215. Further references to this book will be identified
   in the text.
4. The version of the ballad I quote is from *A Pedlar's Pack of Bal-
   lads and Songs*, with illustrative notes by W. H. Logan (Edinburgh:
   William Paterson, 1869), pp. 115–21.

Chapter Five

The Artist as Egoist

IF THE IDEA of the self is based on a denial of the other, then the self can never stand alone. It is eternally dependent on its negative relationship to what it construes to be external and separate. The independence of the self is a fraud. Stephen claims, repeating what Joyce himself had said, that "isolation is the first principle of artistic economy" (*SH*, 33; *CW*, 69); however, Stephen's isolation is clearly a relationship to his society. His solitude is a position in the group: "He was an enigmatic figure in the midst of his shivering society where he enjoyed a reputation" (*SH*, 35). "Stephen may be said to have occupied the position of notable-extraordinary. . . . People began to defer to him, to invite him to their houses and to present serious faces to him. . . . Many risked the peril of rebuff to engage the young eccentric in talk but Stephen preserved a disdainful silence" (*SH*, 39).

This position is sought by Stephen, despite his and the narrator's attempts to place the responsibility elsewhere: "it was natural that the more the youth sought solitude for himself the more his society sought to prevent his purpose. Though he was still in his first year he was considered a personality" (*SH*, 38). The essence of Stephen's egoism is that the relationship must be sought or forced by society, yet at crucial points Stephen himself has to make certain that his reputation is advanced. As was pointed out earlier, Stephen not only enjoys his triumph over the college president's attempted censorship, but also enjoys the reputation it gives him among his fellow students as a "moral Nelson" (*SH*, 99).

73

In fact, lacking a witness, he takes the trouble to give an account of the interview. His argument with his mother, glorified to a battle with orthodoxy, marks his official renunciation of his faith. This renunciation is a liberation from society, yet he must seek out the society of Cranly to justify himself. His last encounter with Emma, when he makes his outrageous and very private proposition, marks the end of another possibility of human relationship (*SH*, 197–99). Although Emma's predictable refusal represents another step toward Stephen's independence and isolation, the whole encounter becomes an "adventure" to add to his legend and to relate to Lynch (*SH*, 200). Each of Stephen's attempts at becoming self-sufficient is canceled by his need for validation of his identity by something outside himself.

Even those passages which emphasize his solitude and his difference betray by their tone the presence of a mirror. Their "poetic" extravagance reveals the fact that they are a form of posing for the benefit of another, provided by the presence of a third-person narrator: "In class, in the hushed library, in the company of other students he would suddenly hear a command to begone, to be alone, a voice agitating the very tympanum of his ear, a flame leaping into divine cerebral life. He would obey the command and wander up and down the streets alone, the fervour of his hope sustained by ejaculations until he felt sure it was useless to wander any more" (*SH*, 30–31).

The contradiction in Stephen's behavior is so persistent that it can be explained only by a basic division in his world such as Gabriel Marcel describes in relation to another egoist, that of George Meredith's novel:

> Burdened with myself, plunged in this disturbing world, sometimes threatening me, sometimes my accomplice, I keep an eager lookout for everything emanating from it which might either soothe or ulcerate the wound I bear within me, which is my *ego*. . . . What then is this anguish, this wound? The answer is that it is above all the experience of being torn by a contradiction between the all which I aspire to possess, to annex, or, still more absurd, to monopolise, and the obscure consciousness that after all I am nothing but an empty void; for, still, I can affirm nothing about myself which would be really myself; nothing, either, which would be permanent; nothing which would be secure

against criticism and the passage of time. Hence the craving to be confirmed from outside, by another; this paradox, by virtue of which even the most self-centered among us looks to others and only to others for his final investiture.[1]

Stephen also is torn between the all which he aspires "to possess, to annex, or . . . to monopolise" and the emptiness of the detached ego. His earliest ambition had been to become a "material Messias. . . . But now such a thought arises in my mind only in moments of great physical weakness" (*SH*, 222). That ambition, however, has only been replaced by a desire to be the spiritual "Messias," to liberate his fellow students (*SH*, 49), his countrymen, to alter the structure of society (*SH*, 147). Moreover, his ridicule, and the narrator's, of the brightest of his fellow students, of the nationalists, and of the priests reveals a jealousy of the fact that they, not he, monopolize the attention of his country. Not another person of intellectual or aesthetic pretensions is allowed to stand in this book. In *A Portrait* Stephen's decision to leave Ireland draws its final strength from his realization that a rival relationship has grown up between E.C. and Cranly (*AP*, 245, 232). E.C. had already become for Stephen a symbol of Ireland (*AP*, 221), a fact which gives depth to Stephen's distaste for her flirtation with the priest and the nationalists both in *Stephen Hero* and *A Portrait*.

Like Marcel's egoist, Stephen also is unable to affirm anything about himself which would be secure from criticism: "Even the value of his own life came into doubt with him. He laid a finger upon every falsehood it contained: [an][2] egoism which proceeded bravely before men to be frighted by the least challenge of the conscience, freedom which would dress the world anew in [the] vestments and usages begotten of enslavement, mastery of an art understood by few which owed its very delicacy to a physical decrepitude, itself the brand and sign of vulgar ardours" (*SH*, 162). The soul-searching of Stephen in this fragmentary novel is not to be underestimated. Despite the bravado with which he is often presented, Stephen's self-doubts are an important element in the book.

Part of Stephen's dismay before a swiftly changing stream of reality is revealed in his meditations on the beach in the "Pro-

teus" and "Scylla and Charybdis" chapters of *Ulysses*. It concerns
the problem of establishing an identity, secure "against the passage of time," and at the same time detaching himself from all external sources of identity: "Molecules all change. I am other I
now" (*U*, 189; see also *AP*, 249). The Stephen of *Stephen Hero*,
however, clings to the fiction of an independent spiritual identity,
separate from the world in which he lives, and separate from, and
thus secure from, even the change of time. That very separateness
from the reality of time turns time into a meaningless succession
of events against which the self is measured and found impotent.
Time is like the aimless chords Stephen plays at the piano when
he is most aware of his own nothingness: "The chords that
floated towards the cobwebs and rubbish and floated vainly to the
dust-strewn windows were the meaningless voices of his pertur-
bation and all they could do was flow in meaningless succession
through all the chambers of sentience. He breathed an air of
tombs" (*SH*, 162).

Here is a basic paradox. Stephen feels an essential difference
from all that he sees around him, yet his sense of himself, in all
its difference, depends for its definition on this negative relationship. His "independence" is dependent on the totally external
otherness of his world, family, fellows. The self stands apart and
is secure from time, and time is a meaningless succession of external events that do not touch him; however, the only definition
of self he can achieve is necessarily in terms of that succession.
This contradiction accounts for the loose temporal organization of
Stephen Hero, which betrays the insecurity of Stephen's identity
and a crippling, unheroic passivity. The book, or at least the fragment we have, is organized merely in terms of a loose chronology,
which is sometimes the only principle of continuity governing
even the paragraph structure.

One rather long paragraph must be made to serve as an example. It begins abruptly, without any relationship to the scene before (a conversation between Stephen and Moynihan about Boc-
caccio) except sequence in time.

> Mr Daedalus had not an acute sense of the rights of private prop-
> erty: he paid rent very rarely. To demand money for eatables

seemed to him just but to expect people to pay for shelter the exorbitant sums which are demanded annually by houseowners in Dublin seemed to him unjust. He had now been a year in his house in Clontarf and for that year he had paid a quarter's rent. The writ which had been first served on him had //contained a legal flaw// and this fact enabled him to prolong his term of occupancy. Just now matters were drawing to a head and he was scouring the city for another house. A private message from a friend in the Sheriff's office gave him exactly five days of grace and every morning he brushed his silk hat very diligently and polished his eyeglasses and went forth humming derisively to offer himself as a bait to landlords. The halldoor was often banged loudly on these occasions as the only possible close of an altercation. The results of the examination had awarded Stephen a mere pass and his father told him very confidentially that he had better look out for some kind of a doss because in a week's time they would be all out on the street. The funds in the house were very low for the new furniture had fetched very little after its transport piecemeal to a pawn-office. Tradesmen who had seen it depart had begun a game of knocking and ringing which was very often followed by the curious eyes of street-urchins. Isabel was lying upstairs in the backroom, day by day growing more wasted and querulous. The doctor came twice a week now and ordered her delicacies. Mrs Daedalus had to set her wits to work to provide even one substantial meal every day and she certainly had no time to spare between accomplishing this feat, appeasing the clamour at the halldoor, parrying her husband's ill-humour and attending on her dying daughter. As for her sons, one was a freethinker, the other surly. //Maurice ate dry bread, muttered maledictions against his father and his father's creditors, practised pushing a heavy flat stone in the garden// and raising and lowering a broken dumb-bell, and trudged to the Bull every day that the tide served. In the evening he wrote his diary or went out for a walk by himself. Stephen wandered about morning, noon and night. The two brothers were not often together [until after]. One dusty summer evening [when] they walked into each other very gravely at a corner and both burst out laughing: and after that they sometimes went for walks together in the evening and discussed the art of literature. (*SH*, 150–51)

The next paragraph moves abruptly to a different topic, Stephen's new relationship with Lynch.

At first it appears that Mr. Daedalus' war with his creditors will be the topic of this paragraph, however discontinuous it is with the paragraphs that precede it. The subject of the trouble over the house, however, is gradually dissipated among details of Stephen's examination, Isabel's illness, Mrs. Daedalus' tasks, until finally it is submerged altogether by the activity of the sons. The only real principle of unity in this paragraph, like so many others in the book, is that which is provided by the phrases "He had now been a year in his house," "Just now," "twice a week now." A summary paragraph of this sort is usually designed to bring forth the background of events and to carry the story forward in time, yet the effect here is a curious kind of stasis and discontinuity, not unlike the paralysis of *Dubliners*. In fact, the whole chapter (22, pp. 144–63) works in the same way. It loosely holds together Stephen's life during one restless, unsettling summer. The fact that it has no tight organization or unity reflects, in a way, Stephen's predicament, his passivity. He is at a loss for direction. The source of change is somehow outside his control and he must wait out the passing of time.

Such loose organization also, of course, reveals the state of the book as we have it, fragmentary, unfinished, not intended to be published. It is not unnatural that it should be a series of disparate scenes, little essays, mood-pieces, loosely joined by shotgun summary paragraphs such as the one quoted above. The difficulty, however, is not simply a matter of Joyce's immaturity as a craftsman. Rather, this discontinuity and fragmentation reveal Joyce's initial problem with his hero and an ambivalence about the location of the self in relation to its world. On the one hand, there is Stephen as Hero, an egoist, an active protagonist like Turpin Hero. He is conceived of as a "personality" who stands apart from his society, an independent spiritual principle. On the other hand, there is the Stephen unable to find himself, passively waiting for the revelation in the passage of time. He is waiting somehow for the gift of freedom and identity from time, totally dependent on time, his world, something outside himself for definition. The secret at the heart of this dualistic structure is that there is no real break between the observing self and the world, but that the self is totally dependent on what it conceives of as external to it.

Stephen's use of his family, his friends, even of his mother is only a more subtle, covert version of Lenehan's use of Corley and

Corley's exploitation of the girl in "Two Gallants." Since his idea of identity is a negation of his society's idea of respectability, it is the negative mirror image of the identity Polly Mooney achieves for herself with her mother's tacit approval and aid through the exploitation of Mr. Doran in "The Boarding House." Actually, Stephen's complex relationship with others is more precisely reflected in Mr. Duffy's ambivalent relationship with Mrs. Sinico. At first he is alone, having achieved a static, negative relationship of denial without freedom. He renounces his society but he does not entirely escape it. He lives on the edge. "Mr James Duffy lived in Chapelizod because he wished to live as far as possible from the city of which he was a citizen and because he found all the other suburbs of Dublin mean, modern and pretentious" (D, 107). His relationship with Mrs. Sinico begins when they meet at a poorly attended concert and it is based on their loneliness and cultural interests in contrast to the concerns of their society. Like so many of Stephen's friendships, their relationship is based on their shared opposition to all the others. Yet Mr. Duffy's friendship with Mrs. Sinico is only another version of his relationship to Dublin. If he has defined himself negatively by his opposition to his society, his interest in Mrs. Sinico is only in the more positive reflection of his idea of himself that she offers: "This union exalted him, wore away the rough edges of his character, emotionalised his mental life. Sometimes he caught himself listening to the sound of his own voice. He thought that in her eyes he would ascend to an angelical stature" (D, 111). Like Stephen, Duffy wants affirmation of his purely spiritual nature. It is that same split between spirit and body noted earlier, the same attempt of the spirit to withdraw from its imprisonment in matter that is revealed again here in Mr. Duffy's desire. His wish to keep their relationship on a purely spiritual plane is what destroys it. He experiences both a pull toward Mrs. Sinico, whose admiration gives him a sense of his own being, and a simultaneous pull away because the definition he seeks insists on his singleness:

> He thought that in her eyes he would ascend to an angelical stature; and, as he attached the fervent nature of his companion more and more closely to him, he heard the strange impersonal voice which he recognized as his own, insisting on the soul's incurable loneliness. We cannot give ourselves, it said: we are our

own. The end of these discourses was that one night during which she had shown every sign of unusual excitement, Mrs Sinico caught up his hand passionately and pressed it to her cheek.

Mr Duffy was very much surprised. Her interpretation of his words disillusioned him. He did not visit her for a week. (D, 111)

Mr. Duffy's desire, like Stephen's, is paradoxical. He seeks "an angelical stature" of spiritual aloofness which, however, is dependent on another person or persons. On another level the same pattern can be seen in the aloofness and impersonality of the narrator of *Dubliners*. There the reader finds the same "impersonal voice . . . insisting on the soul's incurable loneliness. We cannot give ourselves, it said: we are our own."[3] Yet his spiritual superiority and separateness are dependent both on a picture of the world that gives him back his own image and on the reader's recognition of that superiority.

Mr. Duffy's dismay at Mrs. Sinico's response is, in part, a dismay at discovering there is something there beyond a reflection of his own superiority. His rejection of her is a denial of her very being. It is a denial that she is a separate person with thoughts and feelings like his own. He will discover the nature of this denial later: "Why had he withheld life from her? Why had he sentenced her to death?" (D, 117). Her actual death is the realization of what he has already done to her symbolically in refusing to recognize her individuality. His erasure of Mrs. Sinico from his mind and his life has been a kind of murder.

For a while he forgets about her entirely, but when he learns about her death he at first identifies her with the vulgar, commonplace life from which he stands aloof: "His soul's companion! He thought of the hobbling wretches whom he had seen carrying cans and bottles to be filled by the barman. Just God, what an end! Evidently she had been unfit to live, without any strength of purpose, an easy prey to habits, one of the wrecks on which civilisation has been reared" (D, 115).

It had originally been her touch that shocked him into an awareness that she was feeling and thinking something besides what he had attributed to her. Her touch had revealed to him suddenly the existence of another human being, something beyond his power to project. Now as he tries to explain away her death, to see it as proof of her unworthiness, it is again the sense of touch that brings him to the truth: "As the light failed and his memory began to wander he thought her hand touched his" (*D*, 116); "at moments he seemed to feel her voice touch his ear, her hand touch his" (*D*, 117).[4]

Earlier he had seen in her only what had served to confirm his own image of himself, but now he begins to perceive the reality of her life from her point of view: "Now that she was gone he understood how lonely her life must have been, sitting night after night alone in that room. His life would be lonely too until he, too, died, ceased to exist, became a memory—if anyone remembered him" (*D*, 116). Now he identifies himself with her and realizes that his denial of life to her, first by an inability to accept her as a separate consciousness and then by erasing her from his own life, results in a denial of his own reality. There will be no one to grant him existence.

As this fresh sense of her reality fades away, Mr. Duffy experiences the nothingness of the isolated self: "He could not feel her near him in the darkness nor her voice touch his ear. He waited for some minutes listening. He could hear nothing: the night was perfectly silent. He listened again: perfectly silent. He felt that he was alone" (*D*, 117). "A Painful Case" ends here with Mr. Duffy's experience of the full meaning of his solitude. It stops just short of the realization at the end of "The Dead" of the mutual dependency of all the living and the dead and the discovery that, as Ellmann has said, "None has his being alone" (*JJ*, 260). It is perhaps significant that changes in the manuscripts of "A Painful Case" seem to indicate that Joyce found it difficult to write and that he returned to it again in Rome in 1906, just before he conceived of "The Dead." Certainly Joyce's critical attitude toward Mr. Duffy denotes his growing awareness of the problems of spiritual isolation.

The three stories that follow "A Painful Case," both in Joyce's early plan and in the book as it now stands, "Ivy Day," "A Mother," and "Grace," are the ones that concern public life, the politics, art, and religion of Dublin. They are perhaps the most merciless stories in the whole book and the most "objective." That is to say, the narrator stands farthest from the scene he describes and does not identify himself with any single consciousness as he has done in most of the earlier stories. It is as if he shared the solitary position of Mr. Duffy. There is in the narrative no sympathy for any of the characters in these stories, as if Mr. Duffy's failure of sympathy had finally doomed not only him but also the rest of the world to a terrible solitude. Each person is imprisoned by his own petty concerns, unable to communicate with any other person, in fact regarding everyone else as a thing to be used. These stories represent the privacy of "public" life, a life without redemption. "Grace" is a parody of the *Divine Comedy*, more precisely a travesty. Stanislaus has revealed the way his brother planned it according to Dante's tripartite division: "in the underground lavatory, *l'Inferno*; in bed at home convalescing, *il Purgatorio*; in church listening to a sermon, *il Paradiso*."[5] Mr. Kernan climbs to the "heights" of Father Purdon's simoniacal sermon. Misinterpreting Christ's words as setting "as exemplars in the religious life those very worshippers of Mammon who were of all men the least solicitous in matters religious" (*D*, 174), Father Purdon delivers his sermon in the clichés of the commercial world. The *Paradiso* of this story is what Stephen termed the "divinity" of the "obvious" (*SH*, 162, but see also 30), and the narrator's chronicle of this degradation seems to come from the same source as Stephen's vision: "Cemeteries revealed their ineffectual records to him, //records of the lives of all those who with good grace or bad grace had accepted an obvious divinity. The vision of all those failures, and the vision, far more pitiful, of congenital lives, shuffling onwards amid yawn and howl, beset him with evil" (*SH*, 162).

By the end of 1906 both *Dubliners* and *Stephen Hero* had reached the same impasse. Before the addition of "The Dead," *Dubliners* is a picture of total paralysis, sterility, and frustration. Stephen also is arrested in the middle of a broken gesture toward freedom. Both books carry the mood of their own reversal; in a sense, of their own destruction. Both reveal the same emerging pattern. If the self cannot stand alone but is dependent on others, Stephen's desire is fraudulent, self-destructive. The idea of any isolated ego which stands separate from its world is an abstraction and therefore a fiction, since it masks a secret participation in that world. The lonely prison of the Dubliner is an illusion.

Early in "The Dead," Gabriel Conroy has reached the same impasse. Like Stephen, Gabriel suffers the same illusion of self-containment and superiority. Yet, also like Stephen, he is almost totally concerned with other people. First he tries to force the respect of Lily, the maid, with a patronizing statement. Her retort is, to him, direct and deadly accurate: " 'The men that is now is only all palaver and what they can get out of you' " (D, 173). Then to recover control of the situation Gabriel tries to buy her with a Christmas coin.

He shares with Stephen "that ineradicable egoism" in which "he conceived converging to him the deeds and thoughts of his microcosm" (SH, 34), but there is no longer Stephen's hope that this egoism will save him from the world. Gabriel is more vulnerable than Stephen, or at least his dependence on confirmation from outside is more visible:

> He was still discomposed by the girl's bitter and sudden retort. It had cast a gloom over him which he tried to dispel by arranging his cuffs and the bows of his tie. He then took from his waistcoat pocket a little paper and glanced at the headings he had made for his speech. He was undecided about the lines from Robert Browning, for he feared they would be above the heads of his hearers. Some quotation that they would recognize from Shakespeare or from the Melodies would be better. The indelicate clacking of the men's heels and the shuffling of their soles reminded him that their grade of culture differed from his. He would only make himself ridiculous by quoting poetry to them which they could not understand. They would think that he was airing his superior education. He would fail with them just as he had failed with the girl in the pantry. He had taken up a wrong tone. His whole speech was a mistake from first to last, an utter failure. (D, 179)

Although Gabriel has even less self-confidence than Stephen, both are concerned only with what they can get from other people. Stephen's failure to escape Dublin is already implicit in Gabriel's series of little failures that lead up to the total destruction of his egoism at the end of "The Dead."

The doom of Gabriel's idea of self-containment is announced in terms similar to the "malevolent reality" which Stephen imagines is behind the things he fears (AP, 243): "A vague terror seized Gabriel at this answer, as if, at that hour when he had hoped to triumph, some impalpable and vindictive being was coming against him, gathering forces against him in its vague world" (*D*, 229). It is a strange fulfillment of the threat "of some maleficent and sinful being" that the narrator of "The Sisters" associates with the word "paralysis": "It filled me with fear, and yet I longed to be nearer to it and to look upon its deadly work" (*D*, 9). The death Gabriel experiences at the end of the book, however, is not that same paralysis that has appeared in all the earlier stories. It is a death that leads not only to self-knowledge but also to an imaginative involvement with others.

NOTES

1. *Homo Viator*, trans. Emma Craufurd (New York: Harper Torchbooks, 1962), p. 16.
2. For explanation of the markings in passages from *Stephen Hero*, see p. 22, n. 5.
3. See also *AP*, 252, and the voices Stephen hears calling to him as he prepares to leave Ireland: "We are alone."
4. See Hugh Kenner on this point, in *Dublin's Joyce* (Boston: Beacon Press Paperbook, 1962): "Her touch brings otherness, a world of passion lying outside his controlled and swept and tidied world, a denial of the voice that says 'We are our own'" (p. 60).
5. Stanislaus Joyce, "The Background to 'Dubliners,'" *The Listener*, 51 (1954), 526.

Chapter Six

The End of Self-Division

IN ORDER TO WRITE "The Dead," Joyce had to change "in his attitude toward Ireland and so toward the world" (*JJ*, 239, 252).
Richard Ellmann has demonstrated through Joyce's letters many
signs of his change during this period. "The Dead" was planned
during Joyce's unhappy months in Rome in late 1906, begun after his return to Trieste in March, 1907, and completed in early
September. Even earlier, Joyce had periodically shown doubts
about the harshness of the other stories. As early as the summer
of 1905, in the middle of the period when most of the stories
were written, he wondered, in a letter to his brother, whether
they were caricatures: "The Dublin papers will object to my
stories as to a caricature of Dublin life. Do you think there is any
truth in this? At times the spirit directing my pen seems to me so
plainly mischievous that I am almost prepared to let the Dublin
critics have their way" (*Letters*, II, 99).

This wavering attitude accompanied the writing of *Dubliners*
throughout. Ellmann says:

> An ambiguity of motive creeps into his discussion of his book
> and city. "Is it not possible," he asks Stanislaus on September 1,
> 1905, "for a few persons of character and culture to make Dublin
> a capital such as Christiania has become?" His old intention of
> excoriating the city was mixed now with a new one of creating a
> helpful guide to its improvement. Two of the most savage of the
> stories, "The Boarding House" and "Counterparts," left him "un-

commonly well pleased" at first, but a week later, on July 19, he blamed their mercilessness on the Triestine heat: "Many of the frigidities of *The Boarding House* and *Counterparts* were written while the sweat streamed down my face on the handkerchief which protected my collar." (*JJ*, 216; see also *Letters*, II, 98)

By the fall of 1906, when he had begun thinking of "The Dead," these doubts became intense enough to interfere with the writing of other planned stories. His letters began to be filled with defenses of Dublin and Ireland and a questioning of the implications of his stories. "In one letter," says Ellmann, "he suddenly and surprisingly announced that the Irish, because they are the least bureaucratic, are the most civilized people in Europe" (*JJ*, 239; *Letters*, II, 202). In another letter Joyce confessed that he "felt humiliated when anyone attacked his impoverished country" (*JJ*, 263; *Letters*, II, 167). He had begun to feel his exile severely. He wrote to Stanislaus on February 11, 1907, about news of the riots at the Abbey Theatre over Synge's *The Playboy of the Western World*: "This whole affair has upset me. I feel like a man in a house who hears a row in the street and voices he knows shouting but can't get up to see what the hell is going on. It has put me off the story I was 'going to write'—to wit: *The Dead*" (*Letters*, II, 212). Furthermore, Joyce's Trieste lecture of 1907, "Ireland, Island of Saints and Sages" (*CW*, 153), and the three articles for the newspaper *Il Piccolo della Sera*, especially the last one, "Ireland at the Bar," reveal a more defending attitude toward Ireland and a new sympathy for the independence movement. These elements of reconciliation also carried over into Joyce's personal life, and he began to try to mend the breach with his father which had occurred when James eloped from Ireland with Nora Barnacle.

All these facts indicate what is of special importance to this study, that Joyce had become aware in a new way of his own personal involvement in the subject of his stories. This recognition has the greatest importance for the way "The Dead" differs from the other stories. On September 25, 1906, Joyce wrote to his brother:

> I have often confessed to you surprise that there should be anything exceptional in my writing and it is only at moments when

I leave down somebody else's book that it seems to me not so unlikely after all. Sometimes thinking of Ireland it seems to me that I have been unnecessarily harsh. I have reproduced (in *Dubliners* at least) none of the attraction of the city for I have never felt at my ease in any city since I left it, except in Paris. I have not reproduced its ingenuous insularity and its hospitality. The latter "virtue" so far as I can see does not exist elsewhere in Europe. I have not been just to its beauty: for it is more beautiful naturally in my opinion than what I have seen of England, Switzerland, France, Austria or Italy. And yet I know how useless these reflections are. For were I to rewrite the book as G. R. [Grant Richards, his publisher] suggests "in another sense" (where the hell does he get the meaningless phrases he uses) I am sure I should find again what you call the Holy Ghost sitting in the inkbottle and the perverse devil of my literary conscience sitting on the hump of my pen. And after all *Two Gallants*—with the Sunday crowds and the harp in Kildare Street and Lenehan—is an Irish landscape. (*Letters*, II, 166)

"And after all . . ." the stories are true. Joyce is caught by the apparent truth of the stories yet is always uneasy about it, always worried that they do not represent the whole truth. In "The Dead" he will try to reproduce both Ireland's "ingenuous insularity and its hospitality." In fact it is its hospitality that Gabriel Conroy will single out for praise in his Christmas-dinner speech, but that praise will be qualified by its source in Gabriel's rather tangled motives. On the other hand, Gabriel's view of Ireland is very close to that of the earlier stories of the book and to Stephen's in the aborted novel, but by the end of "The Dead" Gabriel will qualify that view almost completely by recognizing his own involvement in his world.[1] Many years later, according to Ellmann, Joyce wrote Georg Goyert about his proposed title for the German translation, that *Dubliners* did not describe the way "they" are in Dublin but the way "we" are (*Letters*, III, 164).

Before leaving Rome to return to Trieste in February of 1907 Joyce went through a very dark time. "My mouth," he wrote, "is full of decayed teeth and my soul of decayed ambition" (*Letters*, II, 216). One letter to Stanislaus, in February, 1907, speaks of the intellectual and creative impasse he had reached. If he was to continue to write, his writing would be more personal "as the continuation of the expression of myself which I now see I began in *Chamber Music*":

I have come to the conclusion that it is about time I made up my mind whether I am to become a writer or a patient Cousins. I foresee that I shall have to do other work as well but to continue as I am at present would certainly mean my mental extinction. It is months since I have written a line and even reading tires me. The interest I took in socialism and the rest has left me. I have gradually slid down until I have ceased to take any interest in any subject. I look at God and his theatre through the eyes of my fellow clerks so that nothing surprises, moves, excites or disgusts me. Nothing of my former mind seems to have remained except a heightened sensitiveness which satisfies itself in the sixty-miles-an-hour pathos of some cinematograph or before some crude Italian gazette-picture. Yet I have certain ideas I would like to give form to: not as a doctrine but as the continuation of the expression of myself which I now see I began in *Chamber Music*. These ideas or instincts or intuitions or impulses may be purely personal. I have no wish to codify myself as anarchist or socialist or reactionary. The spectacle of the procession in honour of the Nolan left me quite cold. I understand that anti-clerical history probably contains a large percentage of lies but this is not enough to drive me back howling to my gods. This state of indifference ought to indicate artistic inclination, but it doesn't. (*Letters*, II, 217)

This letter seems to renounce the earlier claim for the artist as a liberator or savior and to deny impersonality and objectivity as a point of view. The "ideas" or "intuitions" are "purely personal." In this connection, nothing is more pertinent to this study than the indication on Joyce's part of a new attitude toward Ibsen. As was pointed out earlier, Joyce had admired Ibsen's impersonal, godlike vision. Now, however, in his Trieste lecture of 1907 on James Clarence Mangan, Joyce speaks of "the destructive and fiercely self-centered tendency of all of Henrik Ibsen's works" (*CW*, 180). The connection between this new attitude toward Ibsen and *Dubliners* is emphasized by the explanation Joyce gave Stanislaus for not writing the other stories he had planned in Rome: he was too cold to write them. Ibsen, he said, "may have liked that kind of sport" but Joyce intimated that, unlike Ibsen, he was not enough of an "egoarch" (*Letters*, II, 205; see *JJ*, 238).[2]

All these changes of attitude are brought to focus in "The Dead." One critic has pointed out that Gabriel's strange, sleepy

thought at the end—"The time had come for him to set out on his
journey westward" (*D*, 323)—"makes a complete reversal of his
orientation."[3] In a larger sense this reversal holds true for the direction of the whole book and the orientation of its narrator. The
divided structure I have been discussing is fused here.

There is an indication of the nature of this union in the curiously shifting point of view at the very first of "The Dead." Difficult to pin down, it is not the objective, impersonal voice of a
neutral observer. Just as in so many of the earlier stories, the narrator has appropriated the language and rhythms of his characters' speech but not, as in "Eveline," "A Little Cloud," or "Clay,"
that of any single character who is more or less cut off from his surroundings. The narrator at the beginning, rather than being a detached observer, represents something like the spirit of the occasion as experienced by the chief participants. Though his voice
mimics the style of the characters, there is little of the biting irony
of the earlier narrator. At first the narrator suggests the thoughts
of Lily, the maid, but then the voice shifts to the Misses Morkan:

> Lily, the caretaker's daughter, was literally run off her feet.
> Hardly had she brought one gentleman into the little pantry be-
> hind the office on the ground floor and helped him off with his
> overcoat than the wheezy halldoor bell clanged again and she had
> to scamper along the bare hallway to let in another guest. It was
> well for her she had not to attend to the ladies also. But Miss Kate
> and Miss Julia had thought of that and had converted the bathroom
> upstairs into a ladies' dressing-room. Miss Kate and Miss Julia
> were there, gossiping and laughing and fussing, walking after
> each other to the head of the stairs, peering down over the ban-
> isters and calling down to Lily to ask her who had come.
> It was always a great affair, the Misses Morkan's annual dance.
> Everybody who knew them came to it, members of the family,
> old friends of the family, the members of Julia's choir, any of Kate's
> pupils that were grown up enough, and even some of Mary Jane's
> pupils too. Never once had it fallen flat. For years and years it had
> gone off in splendid style, as long as anyone could remember. (*D*,
> 175–76)

The voice is finally indeterminate. It combines the way Lily and
the Misses Morkan might think of the occasion with the way they

might be seen by someone close to them and familiar with their life over a long period. It fuses a curiously external view with the way they might explain themselves:

> Though their life was modest, they believed in eating well; the best of everything: diamond-bone sirloins, three-shilling tea and the best bottled stout. But Lily seldom made a mistake in the orders, so that she got on well with her three mistresses. They were fussy, that was all. But the only thing they would not stand was back answers.
>
> Of course, they had good reason to be fussy on such a night. And then it was long after ten o'clock and yet there was no sign of Gabriel and his wife. Besides they were dreadfully afraid that Freddy Malins might turn up screwed. They would not wish for worlds that any of Mary Jane's pupils should see him under the influence; and when he was like that it was sometimes very hard to manage him. Freddy Malins always came late, but they wondered what could be keeping Gabriel; and that was what brought them every two minutes to the banisters to ask Lily had Gabriel or Freddy come. (D, 176)

With only a little allowance for the irony here, this voice can be seen as representing the awareness of mutual dependency of all the living and the dead that Gabriel Conroy comes to at the end of the story. The irony that is involved has to do with the fussiness of the atmosphere at the beginning of the story. If the narrator's voice represents the kind of group mind of the occasion, it is a feminine mind and this is a woman's world. However vulgar Freddy Malins or Mr. Browne is, theirs is a masculine kind of vulgarity. It must be noted that all of Gabriel's defeats come at the hands of women—Lily, Miss Ivors, his wife. Part of the significance of the contrasts of the present with the past in this story is that a more masculine past has been muffled by the feminine present. The two old spinster sisters preside over this world, just as two other spinster sisters replaced the dead priest in the first story of *Dubliners*.

The point, however, is more complicated than is suggested by this vision of an Ireland robbed of its manhood. Gabriel, however detached and critical of this world, has allowed himself to become its instrument as well as its victim. It is important to notice that he is the elected defender of the social order of the party from whatever disturbance Freddy is expected to cause. He is not an

ideal, poetic, or cultural alternative held by the narrator in contrast to his society as Stephen is in *Stephen Hero* or as he thinks
of himself. In his own fussiness and pedantry, his fear of contact
with anything messy or vulgar or uncalculated, Gabriel is very
like an old woman. Just as the Araby Bazaar was Dublin's idea of
the exotic and did not stand in true opposition to it, Gabriel is
the Misses Morkan's version of the cultural gentleman and he provides no alternative to their world. Both he and the Araby Bazaar,
and even Freddy Malins and Mr. Browne, have their places and
functions in this world. Whatever silliness and sterility it is guilty
of, they share.

This participation in a world Gabriel thinks he stands separate
from is only part of what he discovers at the end of the story.
There is a more total human situation that Gabriel discovers he
shares. Aunt Julia and Aunt Kate are more than allegorical counters in a social satire of Victorian Ireland, certainly more than the
"two ignorant old women" (*D*, 192) Gabriel disdains but uses.
Joyce gives them individualized feelings and personalities and a
human worth that transcends the stereotypes to which Gabriel
reduces them. Aunt Julia, for example, shakes Gabriel's idea of
her with her performance of the song "Arrayed for the Bridal":
"To follow the voice, without looking at the singer's face, was to
feel and share the excitement of swift and secure flight" (*D*, 193).
His recognition of the two women as real persons and of his common humanity with them will be the death of his egoism.

One of the ways "The Dead" differs from the earlier stories of
Dubliners is that Joyce incorporates within the story what has
been the point of view of the narrator toward his characters, or
at least something like that point of view. "The Dead" has a reso-
nance and complexity beyond that of the earlier stories because
it has incorporated their point of view in a larger structure. Like
the earlier narrator, and like Stephen, Gabriel has a sense of a
richer European cultural tradition. He holds this against the culture in which he lives. He has the same sense of the vulgarity and
banality of those around him, a superior vision that "looks down"
on people.

Gabriel also has that same horror of the reality before him as
that earlier self who longed to escape from the defilement of
matter into a pure spiritualism. This longing for escape is em-

bodied in his two visions of the Wellington monument alone in the purity of a fresh snow, a memorial to a dead Irish conqueror on the Continent, a complex symbol of Gabriel's own aspirations: "Gabriel's warm trembling fingers tapped the cold pane of the window. How cool it must be outside! How pleasant it would be to walk out alone, first along by the river and then through the park! The snow would be lying on the branches of the trees and forming a bright cap on the top of the Wellington Monument. How much more pleasant it would be there than at the supper-table!" (D, 192). This passage comes after Gabriel's difficulty with Miss Ivors. The second comes as he stands up to deliver his after-dinner tribute to his aunts: "People, perhaps, were standing in the snow on the quay outside, gazing up at the lighted windows and listening to the waltz music. The air was pure there. In the distance lay the park where the trees were weighted with snow. The Wellington Monument wore a gleaming cap of snow that flashed westward over the white field of Fifteen Acres" (D, 202). The window, symbolic of distance and separation, figures in both passages. In the first, it separates Gabriel from his longed-for escape into a spiritual isolation. In the second, he has imaginatively gone beyond it and is looking back. The indefinite group, "people, perhaps," looking up at the lighted window, seems to suggest a desire to become a part of the festive occasion, a covert desire of the outsider to come inside and become a part of the community, foreshadowing the end of the story.

But Gabriel, however much like the earlier narrator of Dubliners, is clearly not the narrator of "The Dead." He is like a Stephen robbed of heroism and placed in a true relationship to his society by a larger vision. One of the easiest ways to see the change that "The Dead" represents in Joyce's work is to contrast the scene of Gabriel's argument with Molly Ivors with Stephen's triumph over the nationalistic Mr. Heffernan at Mullinger in one of the earliest episodes of Stephen Hero remaining (SH, 246–49). In both cases the subject is the same, the Irish language and the desirability of knowing Ireland, particularly country Ireland, as opposed to an interest in Continental culture. In the Stephen Hero episode Stephen is performing under approval of his god-father, Mr. Fulham, whose social position ensures his success.

Stephen pompously gives a religious argument that reduces Heffernan to submission: "Jesus was not of your opinion, Mr Heffernan, said Stephen," adding in explanation that "the ideal presented to mankind by Jesus is one of self-denial, of purity, and of solitude; the ideal you present to us is one of revenge, of passion and of immersion in worldly affairs" (*SH*, 248). He clinches his argument finally by twisting Mr. Heffernan's words in a way that suggests he has been disrespectful to Mr. Fulham:

> —You can be a patriot, Mr Heffernan, said Stephen, without accusing those who do not agree with you of irreligion.
> —I never accused . . .
> —Come now, said Mr Fulham genially, we all understand each other.
> Stephen had enjoyed this little skirmish: it had been a pastime for him to turn the guns of orthodoxy upon the orthodox ranks and see how they would stand the fire. Mr Heffernan seemed to him a typical Irishman of the provinces. (*SH*, 249)

The episode is one of great sport for Stephen. He is able to exploit a safe situation and use arguments he does not really believe to please Mr. Fulham, make a fool of Mr. Heffernan, and prove himself superior. The episode would be a fitting fantasy for Gabriel and Gabriel's defeat a nightmare for Stephen.

> "And haven't you your own language to keep in touch with— Irish?" asked Miss Ivors.
> "Well," said Gabriel, "if it comes to that, you know, Irish is not my language."
> Their neighbors had turned to listen to the cross-examination. Gabriel glanced right and left nervously and tried to keep his good humour under the ordeal which was making a blush invade his forehead.
> "And haven't you your own land to visit," continued Miss Ivors, "that you know nothing of, your own people, and your own country?" (*D*, 189)

Here Stephen's situation is reversed. It is Gabriel who is made to feel self-conscious and nervous of the onlookers. Stephen's bold retort to Mr. Heffernan—"My own mind is more interesting to me than the entire country" (*SH*, 248)—is ironically echoed in Gabriel's final, frustrated reply:

> "O, to tell you the truth," retorted Gabriel suddenly, "I'm sick of my own country, sick of it!"
>
> "Why?" asked Miss Ivors.
>
> Gabriel did not answer for his retort had heated him.
>
> "Why?" repeated Miss Ivors.
>
> They had to go visiting together and, as he had not answered her, Miss Ivors said warmly:
>
> "Of course, you've no answer."
>
> Gabriel tried to cover his agitation by taking part in the dance with great energy. (D, 189–90)

It is interesting to speculate whether Stephen could have answered the same question. That Gabriel and Miss Ivors "had to go visiting together" is part of the larger irony of this scene. The whole argument takes place while they are participating in a dance in which the "visit" is a figure. Ironically, the phrase also suggests her invitation to Gabriel that he and Gretta join an excursion to the West of Ireland: an invitation that starts the argument. The fact that they "had to go visiting together" foreshadows Gabriel's recognition at the end of the story that "the time had come for him to set out on his journey westward" (D, 223). There is even more significance in the dance Gabriel shares with Miss Ivors. Dance is a traditional symbol for harmony and union. In this way, of course, it is in ironic contrast to the argument that takes place during it. Beyond that, however, the dance suggests the larger human order in which Gabriel participates without realizing it. The dance is the occasion of a contact with Miss Ivors that belies her rancor toward Gabriel, or at least, his interpretation of it. It seems to him that "she had tried to make him ridiculous before people, heckling him and staring at him with her rabbit's eyes" (D, 190). But when he remembers that she had praised his review, even though it was for a "West Briton" paper, he wonders, "Was she sincere? Had she really any life of her own behind all her propagandism?" (D, 192).

He has forgotten, although the reader is not meant to, the way the dance has enabled Miss Ivors to qualify her teasing of Gabriel: "When their turn to cross had come he was still perplexed and inattentive. Miss Ivors promptly *took his hand in a warm grasp* and said in a soft friendly tone: 'Of course, I was only joking. Come, we cross now' " (D, 183; my italics). Again at the end of the argument: "When they met in the long chain he was surprised *to feel his hand firmly pressed.* She looked at him from under her brows for a moment quizzically until he smiled" (*D*, 190; my italics). Gabriel, who so carefully has insulated himself from contact with reality—his goloshes—is constantly discovering his defenses broken down.[4] This is the importance of what William York Tindall has pointed out as the motif of the touch in this story.[5] The expressive touch of Molly Ivors' hand is the surest sign of a personal life of her own beyond any labeling of her by Gabriel. She exists in her own right, beyond Gabriel's use of her either to salve or threaten his ego. Throughout the story he is "touched" by something outside himself until at the end he recognizes his wife's otherness and separate inwardness. Paradoxically he must recognize that otherness before he becomes aware of what he shares with it. This recognition is presaged by the touch from Molly Ivors, and the harmony of the dance which makes the touch possible.

Gabriel's attempt to exploit other people always brings results he does not expect. The first example is Lily's unexpected response to his condescending familiarity. He thinks he knows everyone, only to be surprised by indications of separate wills and feelings. He is surprised by Miss Ivors' attack (*D*, 188, 192), surprised by his aunt's singing, surprised even by Freddy Malins' paying him back the pound he lent him (*D*, 217). He is totally routed by the discovery that his wife has an inner life he never suspected. But the truth is there all along. He carefully designs his after-dinner speech to make a point against Miss Ivors, who defeats him again by leaving before he delivers it. His intended criticism of her applies just as much to himself: " 'The generation which is now on the wane among us may have had its faults but for my part I think it had certain qualities of hospitality, of humour, of humanity, which the new and very serious and hypereducated generation that is growing up around us seems to me to lack.' Very good: that was one for Miss Ivors" (*D*, 192). Gabriel, more than Miss Ivors, has shown a lack of hospitality, humor, and humanity. The speech is rank hypocrisy as far as he is concerned, calculated for effect—"what did he care that his aunts were only two ignorant old women?" (*D*, 192). Yet it represents the truth Joyce underlined in his letter to Stanislaus about the "virtues" of Ireland, the truth that *Dubliners* had neglected and that this story demonstrates. Moreover, the speech, however insincere, deeply touches those it is meant to honor.

Gabriel carefully suppresses all his spontaneous impulses toward his wife in the last part of the story and carefully plans a stagy scene:

> When the others had gone away, when he and she were in the room in the hotel, then they would be alone together. He would call her softly:
> "Gretta!"
> Perhaps she would not hear at once: she would be undressing. Then something in his voice would strike her. She would turn and look at him. . . . (*D*, 214)

When the scene is acted out, however, she fails to respond to his manipulation. It is only a bid for time that causes him to tell her about Freddy and the loaned pound. When she expresses interest in that, he has "to restrain himself from breaking out into brutal language about the sottish Malins and his pound" (*D*, 217). Yet it is this story that unexpectedly brings her to him: "She stood before him for an instant looking at him strangely. Then, suddenly raising herself on tiptoe and resting her hands lightly on his shoulders, she kissed him. 'You are a very generous person, Gabriel,' she said" (*D*, 217). Again, an unexpected response, and an ironic one, for Gabriel has seemed anything but a generous person, although he will offer real generosity soon (*D*, 223).

Gabriel's treatment of Gretta is the epitome of his treatment of everyone else: "He longed to be master of her strange mood" (*D*, 217). His failure with her is the climax of all his earlier failures to annex other people to his own ego. The discovery that Gretta has memories and feelings he never suspected leads first of all to a purgative self-knowledge. First he sees himself in the mirror: "As he passed in the way of the cheval-glass he caught sight of himself in full length, his broad, well-filled shirt-front, the face whose expression always puzzled him when he saw it in a mirror, and his glimmering gilt-rimmed eyeglasses" (*D*, 218). When she has begun to tell about Michael Furey, the image in the looking-glass comes clear: "A shameful consciousness of his own person assailed him. He saw himself as a ludicrous figure, acting as a pennyboy for his aunts, a nervous, well-meaning sentimentalist, orating to vulgarians and idealising his own clownish lusts, the pitiable fatuous fellow he had caught a glimpse of in the mirror" (*D*, 220).

This mirror glimpse of himself seems objective, for it is a curiously external vision. It does him no more justice, however, than his scathing view of other people does them. It is only part of the truth, like Stephen's moment of despair during his sister's fatal illness. It is important for Gabriel to see himself in this way, however, because it represents a break in his self-possession and leads to the discovery that the secret life of others might be like his own. This external picture of himself is related to the discovery of the part he might play in Gretta's mind: "While he had been full of memories of their secret life together, full of tenderness and joy and desire, she had been comparing him in her mind with another" (*D*, 219). Like Stephen, Gabriel fears most this comparison, for it means not only a loss of his singularity, his uniqueness, but also the failure of his self-possession. It means there is a part of him that belongs to other people to do with mentally what they want, and this implies a loss of control over his relationships. Recognizing this is another step toward the discovery of his dependence on other people, for it is the discovery of a radical vulnerability of the ego. The possibility that this external aspect of himself could be an object for comparison in the mind of Gretta leads to the recognition of that aspect of himself as himself.

By acknowledging Gretta's power, he is put in the position of judging himself as an object, in the way that he has passed judgment on others. The result of seeing himself as others see him is shame: "Instinctively he turned his back more to the light lest she might see the shame that burned upon his forehead" (*D*, 220). The shame is the shame of the way he appears to Gretta, and therefore is an acknowledgment of her power and the inescapable power of others over him. In a sense the shame brought about by the other is as exaggerated as the pride Gabriel derives in his use of others as a reflection and amplifier of his ego. It is the opposite extreme from his previous relationship with them. Yet there is a difference in this scene because it is his first real recognition of the inner life of other people.

First, there is a breakdown of what Gabriel had imagined as "their secret life together" (*D*, 213). When she comes to him with the kiss for his generosity to Freddy Malins he supposes for a moment she has responded to his calculated manipulations of her: "Just when he was wishing for it she had come to him of her own accord. Perhaps her thoughts had been running with his. Perhaps she had felt the impetuous desire that was in him, and then the yielding mood had come upon her. Now that she had fallen to him so easily, he wondered why he had been so diffident" (*D*, 217–18). When she reveals her thoughts and memories to him, however, this whole imagined structure falls apart.

This revelation, though, is not the discovery that everyone is alone and cut off from everyone else, a solitary prisoner of the self. The revelation does not lead to a hopeless solipsism. The discovery that his wife is a stranger to him is a real contact with another subjectivity. Gabriel discovers another person: "He watched her while she slept, as though he and she had never lived together as man and wife. His curious eyes rested long upon her face and on her hair: and, as he thought of what she must have been then, in that first time of her first girlish beauty, a strange, friendly pity for her entered his soul" (*D*, 222).

Gabriel acknowledges that discovery of her separateness which marks the end of his attempt to control or manipulate her. It is an act of respect toward her separate being: "Gabriel held her hand for a moment longer, irresolutely, and then, shy of intruding on her grief, let it fall gently and walked quietly to the window" (*D*, 222).[6] At the same time Gabriel's discovery of Gretta extends to other people and to an imaginative projection of his involvement with them:

> Poor Aunt Julia! She, too, would soon be a shade with the shade of Patrick Morkan and his horse. He had caught that haggard look upon her face for a moment when she was singing *Arrayed for the Bridal*. Soon, perhaps, he would be sitting in that same drawing-room, dressed in black, his silk hat on his knees. The blinds would be drawn down and Aunt Kate would be sitting be-

side him, crying and blowing her nose and telling him how Julia
had died. He would cast about in his mind for some words that
might console her, and would find only lame and useless ones. Yes,
yes: that would happen very soon.

The air of the room chilled his shoulders. He stretched himself
cautiously along under the sheets and lay down beside his wife.
One by one, they were all becoming shades. Better pass boldly
into that other world, in the full glory of some passion, than fade
and wither dismally with age. He thought of how she who lay
beside him had locked in her heart for so many years that image
of her lover's eyes when he had told her that he did not wish to
live.

Generous tears filled Gabriel's eyes. He had never felt like that
himself towards any woman, but he knew that such a feeling must
be love. (*D*, 222–23)

Gabriel's discovery of other people and his new sympathy for
them is an imaginative identification with their thoughts and feelings. Paradoxically the breakdown of his illusion of control over
them is a breakdown of the barriers between them and leads to a
new mode of knowledge. It is significant that the death of egoism
coincides with this memory of the death of a romantic young man,
not unlike Stephen as a dreamy, melancholy poet.

He recognizes Furey's feeling, although he "had never felt like
that himself." But, while Gabriel thinks of his own inadequacy,
he too has surrendered himself to another person. He has experienced a sympathy so profound it must be called love.

Gabriel's relinquishing of his identity is experienced as a kind
of death. Ellmann describes it very well:

> Gabriel is conceding and relinquishing a good deal—his sense
> of the importance of civilized thinking, of continental tastes, of
> all those tepid but nice distinctions on which he has prided him-
> self. The bubble of his self-possession is pricked; he no longer
> possesses himself, and not to possess oneself is in a way a kind of
> death. It is a self-abandonment not unlike Furey's, and through
> Gabriel's mind runs the imagery of Calvary. . . . To some extent
> Gabriel too is dying for her, in giving up what he has most valued
> in himself, all that holds him apart from the simpler people at the
> party. (*JJ*, 258–59)

The idea of the ego is based on a division of the world. It is defined by contrast to all else that is. The ego is figure and the world

is ground. This separation gives rise to the illusion that the two are really independent and that the ego is complete and self-sufficient. Gabriel's discovery that "he no longer possesses himself" is the revelation of that illusion. Self and world cannot be separated but belong to each other.

Gabriel's sacrifice of his aspiration of self-containment is described as a flowing out into the world from which he has been separated: "His own identity was fading out into a grey impalpable world: the solid world itself, which these dead had one time reared and lived in, was dissolving and dwindling" (*D*, 223). Just as the idea of a separate ego or identity is an illusion, so too is the notion of an external and self-contained world. The self is in the world and the world is in the self. The two exist in an overlapping relationship and it is impossible to fix a boundary between them.

From the standpoint of the relationship between the self and others, the solidity of the external world is illusory in another sense. The world is described as a creation of "these dead," i.e., the human community of the past: "the solid world itself, which those dead had one time *reared* and lived in" (*D*, 223; my italics). The self and other, mutually dependent, have as their mutual project the creation of a world. The concept of dualistic realism, which was the starting point of this study, has been discarded. For Joyce, the concept is false because it is based on a reflection. Self, other, and world are overlapping parts of one structure. Gabriel's journey "westward," then, is a movement not only toward the past but toward a primitive source of life. It is a journey back to all that the self has denied.

The resignation of the separate ego is a fall from an aloof position, a fall into the world. Gabriel's fall, since it resolves the dualistic structure of *Dubliners*, is also the narrator's. The ending of "The Dead" transforms the nature of the book from the cold, despairing irony which the ending of "Grace" would have given it. In the last three stories before "The Dead," the public life of Dublin is shown at its most tawdry and banal. The narrator, at the greatest distance from his world, reveals the complete debasement of all that is significant in politics, art, and religion. In effect, the narrator is Gabriel at the Morkans' although he is an even more brutal observer than Gabriel. Gabriel's reversal, his recognition of his involvement in his world, implies a similar change in the narrator. What this reversal does is to make dramatic the narrative development of the book. More than a story about Dubliners, it enacts the development toward self-knowledge of the narrator himself.

Joyce began by identifying himself with the position of the narrator, as his letters to Grant Richards reveal. The first three stories of the book are first-person narrations, which Joyce characterized in a letter to Stanislaus as "stories of my childhood" (*Letters*, II, 111). These stories establish the narrator's solitary position as an observer separated from his world. As the stories progress, the "I" drops away and only the external world is presented, the implicit act of observation of a detached, ironic observer. This division reaches its most severe form in "*Ivy Day in the Committee Room, A Mother* and the last story of the book [*Grace*] which are stories of public life in Dublin." The most "public" of the stories are those in which the narrator is most "private," that is, hidden and impersonal. The effect of "The Dead," however, since it reverses the meaning given to the life of the Dubliners, is to bring the narrator of the other stories out of hiding. It makes the distance of the narrator from the world he is observing the subject of the story. Because it reverses the meaning of that distance, "The Dead" breaks the link between Joyce and the narrator of the earlier stories and adds another kind of irony to their narration. In 1910 Joyce underlined this separation in a letter to G. Molyneux Palmer: "I hope it [*Dubliners*] may interest you though I don't think you will recognize me in it at first glance as it is somewhat bitter and sordid" (*Letters*, I, 70). This change in Joyce's relationship to *Dubliners* brings to the surface the development of the narrator. The narrator, rather than standing outside, becomes a fictional role developing within the book. Gabriel's surrender of the independence of his ego coincides with the abandonment of the notion of a narrator independent of the world he speaks. Instead the narrator is revealed as an essential characteristic of that world.

In its development *Dubliners* is a concrete version of that aesthetic process Stephen describes in *A Portrait*: "The simplest epical form is seen emerging out of lyrical literature when the artist prolongs and broods upon himself as the centre of an epical event and this form progresses till the centre of emotional gravity is equidistant from the artist himself and from others. The narrative is no longer purely personal. The personality of the artist passes into the narration itself, flowing round and round the persons and the action like a vital sea. This progress you will see easily in that old English ballad *Turpin Hero* which begins in the first person and ends in the third person" (*AP*, 215).

The ending of "The Dead" looks forward to the at-one-ment of "Stephen-Blephen" and "Bloom-Stoom" in the "Ithaca" chapter of *Ulysses*, to Molly's final affirmation as she drifts into sleep at the end of that book, and to Anna Livia's dying speech as she merges with her ocean father at the end of *Finnegans Wake*. The implications of Gabriel's union with others and the dissolution of the solid world in "The Dead" are far-reaching in Joyce's later fiction. The solid world at the beginning of *Ulysses* also dissolves and merges with a series of fictional narrators as does the barrier between the internal and external lives of its characters. *Finnegans Wake* is a never-ending cycle of shifting identities, a constant metamorphosis of characters and narrators. I should add that the ending of "The Dead" is actually less positive than I have implied. Gabriel's discovery is a painful one, and the transformation of his world is accompanied by the imagery of death.

More immediately, "The Dead" provided Joyce with the resolution of the problem of *Stephen Hero*. His decision to scrap the book came just as he was finishing "The Dead." Ellmann writes:

> On September 8 [1907] he informed Stanislaus that as soon as he had completed the story he would rewrite *Stephen Hero* completely. "He told me," Stanislaus noted in his diary, "he would omit all the first chapters and begin with Stephen, whom he will call Daly, going to school and that he would write the book in five chapters—long chapters." The use of the name Dedalus must have seemed for the moment too strange, but it is hard to conceive of Joyce's hero with the name Daly. In the plan for five chapters, however, Joyce had evidently hit upon the book's final structure.
>
> By November 29 Joyce had finished revising his first chapter. He continued to work at his novel until April 8, 1908, by which time he had finished the third chapter. (*JJ*, 274)

Stephen Hero ends also, then, with the writing of "The Dead."
The implication is that, like *Dubliners*, it also ends in the narrator's coming to self-awareness, but in this case that self-awareness
results in rejection of its contradictions. *Stephen Hero* is replaced
by a form which contains those contradictions, reveals them and
gives them a different meaning.

NOTES

1. Joyce's use of his own experiences for Gabriel's in this story is also
   interesting. There is a suggestion of an identification with Gabriel
   (see *JJ*, 252, 255–56). There is also Joyce's letter to Nora on August
   22, 1909: "Do you remember the three adjectives I have used in
   'The Dead' in speaking of *your* body. They are these: 'musical and
   strange and perfumed'" (*Letters*, II, 239; my italics). This is the
   way Gabriel thinks of Gretta's body in "The Dead" (*D*, 215). In
   another letter to Nora, Joyce referred to "The Lass of Aughrim" as
   "your song" (*Letters*, II, 242).
2. The other stories were to be titled "The Last Supper," "The Street,"
   "Vengeance," "At Bay," and "Catharsis." It was also during this
   period that Joyce began to think of a story entitled "Ulysses" to
   add to the *Dubliners* group. See *JJ*, 238–39.
3. Brendan P. O Hehir, "Structural Symbol in Joyce's 'The Dead,'"
   in *Joyce's The Dead*, ed. William T. Moynihan (Boston: Allyn and
   Bacon, 1965), p. 130, reprinted from *Twentieth Century Literature*,
   3 (April, 1957), 3–13.
4. Gabriel's goloshes might be considered a satiric version of Stephen's
   "enigma of a manner" carefully constructed for defense (*Workshop*, 61; *SH*, 27). See also O Hehir on the goloshes, "Structural
   Symbol," pp. 120–22, and William York Tindall, *The Literary Symbol* (Bloomington: Indiana University Midland Book, 1955), p. 226.
5. *A Reader's Guide to James Joyce* (New York: The Noonday Press,
   1959), p. 48.
6. Cf. Stephen's new-found liking for E. C. after he has given up trying to annex her to his soul: "Yes, I liked her today. A little or much?
   Don't know. I liked her and it seems a new feeling to me. Then, in
   that case, all the rest, all that I thought I thought and all that I felt
   I felt, all the rest before now, in fact . . . O, give it up, old chap!
   Sleep it off!" (*AP*, 252).

III
Ricorso

Chapter Seven

The Artist as a Young Man

IN HIS 1904 AUTOBIOGRAPHICAL ESSAY "A Portrait of the Artist" Joyce gives this example of his young spirituality: "His training had early developed a very lively sense of spiritual obligations at the expense of what is called 'common sense.' He ran through his measure like a spendthrift saint, astonishing many by ejaculatory fervours, offending many by airs of the cloister. One day in a wood near Malahide a labourer had marvelled to see a boy of fifteen praying in an ecstasy of Oriental posture" (*Workshop*, 60). Despite the irony directed at himself, the anecdote is as critical of the hypocrisy of ordinary religiousness as it is of his own unrealistic zeal. Joyce goes on to underline this point: "It was indeed a long time before this boy understood the nature of that most marketable goodness which makes it possible to give comfortable assent to propositions without ordering one's life in accordance with them" (*Workshop*, 60).

The anecdote appears again in *Stephen Hero*. The same contrast is made and the same conclusion drawn from it, this time at the expense of the conventional spirituality of Emma Clery:

> She seemed to conform to the Catholic belief, to obey the commandments and the precepts. By all outward signs he was compelled to esteem her holy. But he could not so stultify himself as to misread the gleam in her eyes as holy or to interpret the [motions][1] rise and fall of her bosom as a movement of a sacred intention. He thought of his own [fervid religiousness] spendthrift

> religiousness and airs of the cloister, he remembered having as-
> tonished a labourer in a wood near Malahide by an ecstasy of
> Oriental posture and no more than half-conscious under the in-
> fluence of her charm he wondered whether the God of the Roman
> Catholics would put him into hell because he had failed to under-
> stand that most marketable goodness which makes it possible to
> give comfortable assent to propositions without in the least order-
> ing one's life in accordance with them and had failed to appreciate
> the digestive value of the sacraments. (*SH*, 156)

In both cases an important aspect of the story is the effect the
sight of the boy praying in the woods had on "a labourer." In the
essay version he "marvelled to see" the boy; in the novel he is
"astonished" by him. It is a juxtaposition of the boy's exotic posture (and posturing) against the ordinariness of a worldly person.

In *A Portrait of the Artist as a Young Man* the anecdote is repeated. This time the hypocrisy of the other has dropped out of
the scene altogether, and it is Stephen who is made to feel uncom-
fortable by an interruption of his solitary dreaming. Stephen remembers the incident in relationship to Cranly's

> harsh comments, the sudden intrusions of rude speech with which
> he had shattered so often Stephen's ardent wayward confes-
> sions[.] Stephen had forgiven freely for he had found this rude-
> ness also in himself towards himself. And he remembered an
> evening when he had dismounted from a borrowed creaking bi-
> cycle to pray to God in a wood near Malahide. He had lifted up
> his arms and spoken in ecstasy to the sombre nave of the trees,
> knowing that he stood on holy ground and in a holy hour. And
> when two constabularymen had come into sight round a bend in
> the gloomy road he had broken off his prayer to whistle loudly an
> air from the last pantomime. (*AP*, 232)

The "borrowed creaking bicycle," the "two constabularymen,"
and the "air from the last pantomime" are comic additions to the
anecdote. This time the anecdote is told at the expense of Stephen's
own self-consciousness. He is no longer the heroic outlaw who exposes the falsity of the world. The division is still there, a sharp
discrepancy between the "holy ground . . . in a holy hour" and the
world of constabularymen. Stephen is caught between two irreconcilable actions: "to pray to God" and to justify himself to men

of the world by more acceptable behavior. The farcical juxtaposition of praying and whistling loudly a music-hall melody measures the distance between two worlds Stephen is unable to unite. The hidden theme of the earlier works moves to the foreground in *A Portrait*. Here in this anecdote is Stephen's realization that validation of his being from a transcendent spiritual realm is impossible. The encounter with the other that violates the self is a rude awakening to reality.

As Dorothy Van Ghent, among others, has demonstrated, each chapter moves from a chaos of impressions to a moment of decision which creates order.[2] That moment of order is then dissipated or shattered by a fresh encounter with the world in the next chapter. The elements of the order are always the same. As many critics have pointed out, they are derived from the pattern set by the first page and a half. These motifs, however, take on a greater density of meaning in each chapter as Stephen's mind grows in complexity and as these motifs accrete nuances and allusiveness in Stephen's encounters with the world.

The movement of the book is based on this encounter with otherness that destroys the order within the self and is described in those passages about the soul's going forth to encounter reality. It is in these terms that Stephen thinks of his experiences with the prostitutes:

> It was his own soul going forth to experience, unfolding itself sin by sin, spreading abroad the balefire of its burning stars and folding back upon itself, fading slowly, quenching its own lights and fires. . . .
> . . . At his first violent sin he had felt a wave of vitality pass out of him and had feared to find his body or his soul maimed by the excess. Instead the vital wave had carried him on its bosom out of himself and back again when it receded: and no part of body or soul had been maimed but a dark peace had been established between them. (*AP*, 103)

After his religious phase the same terms are used to describe Stephen's feeling that he is incapable of the encounter: "In vague sacrificial or sacramental acts alone his will seemed drawn to go forth to encounter reality: and it was partly the absence of an appointed rite which had always constrained him to inaction whether he had allowed silence to cover his anger or pride or had suffered only an embrace he longed to give" (AP, 159).

The girl Stephen sees on the beach at the end of the fourth chapter appears to him as an "angel of mortal youth and beauty, an envoy from the fair courts of life, to throw open before him in an instant of ecstasy the gates of all the ways of error and glory" (AP, 172). The word "ecstasy" is precise, for again it is a confrontation with otherness that calls him out of himself: "On and on and on and on he strode, far out over the sands, singing wildly to the sea, crying to greet the advent of the life that had cried to him. Her image had passed into his soul for ever and no word had broken the holy silence of his ecstasy. Her eyes had called to him and his soul had leaped at the call" (AP, 172). Stephen's soul (in a description that brings to mind Gabriel at the end of "The Dead") "was swooning into some new world, fantastic, dim, uncertain, as under sea, traversed by cloudy shapes and beings" (AP, 172).

Again at the end of the novel Stephen uses the phrase about the encounter with reality in his journal to describe his feelings at his exile: "Mother is putting my new secondhand clothes in order. She prays now, she says, that I may learn in my own life and away from home and friends what the heart is and what it feels. Amen. So be it. Welcome, O life! I go to encounter for the millionth time the reality of experience and to forge in the smithy of my soul the uncreated conscience of my race" (AP, 252–53).

This passage is full of hope for Stephen's Daedalian flight, but because of the pattern of the other chapters the reader knows that the flight will be followed by a fall. In the pattern that has been established throughout the novel, this is the instant of decision that creates only a temporary order, one soon to be broken by a fresh encounter. Here, however, Stephen has made a decision for that encounter. He has accepted the necessity of the fall he had foreseen when he decided against becoming a Jesuit: "He would fall. He had not yet fallen but he would fall silently, in an instant. Not to fall was too hard, too hard: and he felt the silent lapse of his soul, as it would be at some instant to come, falling, falling but not yet fallen, still unfallen but about to fall" (AP, 162).

It is a prophecy of the fall Stephen remembers in Ulysses, in words echoing the final words of A Portrait: "Fabulous artificer,

the hawklike man. You flew. Whereto? Newhaven-Dieppe, steer-
age passenger. Paris and back. Lapwing. Icarus. *Pater, ait*. Sea-
bedabbled, fallen, weltering. Lapwing you are" (*U*, 210). He even
foresees in *A Portrait* something of the nature of this fall into the
world: "The faint sour stink of rotted cabbages came towards him
from the kitchen gardens on the rising ground above the river.
He smiled to think that it was this disorder, the misrule and con-
fusion of his father's house and the stagnation of vegetable life,
which was to win the day in his soul" (*AP*, 162). It is the beginning
of an acceptance of "the odour of ashpits and old weeds and offal"
which hangs around the stories of *Dubliners*. The ending of *A
Portrait* is not, of course, the anticipation of failure. The novel
ends on a high note with Stephen's commitment to art and his acceptance of exile. This will not change in *Ulysses*, where Stephen
moves toward new levels of understanding.

At the beginning of *A Portrait* at Clongowes, Stephen is a small,
weak boy, alone and without a place in a frightening chaos:

> He kept on the fringe of his line, out of sight of his prefect, out of
> the reach of the rude feet, feigning to run now and then. He felt
> his body small and weak amid the throng of players and his eyes
> were weak and watery. . . . He was caught in the whirl of a scrim-
> mage and, fearful of the flashing eyes and muddy boots, bent down
> to look through the legs. The fellows were struggling and groan-
> ing and their legs were rubbing and kicking and stamping. Then
> Jack Lawton's yellow boots dodged out the ball and all the other
> boots and legs ran after. (*AP*, 8–10)

Even his identity, mysterious to himself, is in question:

> —What is your name?
> Stephen had answered:
> —Stephen Dedalus.
> Then Nasty Roche had said:
> —What kind of a name is that?

Although Stephen tries to stay apart from the world around him
it continues to threaten him. Although he thought that "it was
best to hide out of the way because when you were small and
young you could often escape that way" (*AP*, 55), Wells shoulders him into the cold, slimy water of the ditch and Father Dolan,

accusing him of malingering, pandies his hands. Stephen's first attempt to create order in this world is his appeal to a higher authority against Father Dolan's injustice. Alone, he walks up the stairs, passing "along the narrow dark corridor" (*AP*, 53), under the portraits of the saints who intercede in heaven for those of this world. Stephen's contact with the rector is one of those meetings in the book described in terms of touch, suggestive of contact with others: "The rector held his hand across the side of the desk where the skull was and Stephen, placing his hand in it for a moment, felt a cool moist palm" (*AP*, 38). The reassurance the rector gives him is later revealed to be a falsity and becomes a new source of shame (*AP*, 72). For the moment, however, it seems to give order to Stephen's world and by making him a hero among his schoolmates it gives him an identity: "He was alone. He was happy and free" (*AP*, 59).

More precisely, Stephen's successful appeal to higher authority ratifies the hierarchical order he had composed on the flyleaf of his geography book:

Stephen Dedalus
Class of Elements
Clongowes Wood College
Sallins
County Kildare
Ireland
Europe
The World
The Universe

That was in his writing: and Fleming one night for a cod had written on the opposite page:

Stephen Dedalus is my name,
Ireland is my nation.
Clongowes is my dwellingplace
And heaven my expectation.
(*AP*, 15-16)

This is not only an order which assures Stephen of a definite place and an identity, but it is also one with links between places, steps in the chain, and it gives assurance of a connection between the finite and the infinitely great—"heaven." It is this order which, like the successful appeal to the rector, promises justice on earth and an answer to the prayer to a distant God: "*Incline unto our aid, O God! | O Lord, make haste to help us!*" (AP, 17); "*Visit, we beseech Thee, O Lord, this habitation and drive away from it all the snares of the enemy*" (AP, 18), prayers which Stephen offers "against the dark outside under the trees" (AP, 18).³

This hierarchical order is deceptive, however, because it seems to link realms which in reality cannot hold together. It is a spurious order which conceals a series of rifts in the universe. In this way it is like the lines of "poetry" in Stephen's spelling book which are really "only sentences to learn the spelling from":

> *Wolsey died in Leicester Abbey*
> *Where the abbots buried him.*
> *Canker is a disease of plants,*
> *Cancer one of animals.*
> (*AP*, 10)

Like these sentences, the places in Stephen's "great chain of being" are discrete realms with no real connection with one another. They constantly demand of Stephen an "either/or" answer which, because it cuts the universe in half, can never be satisfactory. The apparent order of the universe conceals a mystery for Stephen like Wells's question, which can be satisfied by neither of the two possible answers:

> —Tell us, Dedalus, do you kiss your mother before you go to bed?
> Stephen answered:
> —I do.
> Wells turned to the other fellows and said:
> —O, I say, here's a fellow says he kisses his mother every night before he goes to bed.
> The other fellows stopped their game and turned round, laughing. Stephen blushed under their eyes and said:
> —I do not.
> Wells said:
> —O, I say, here's a fellow says he doesn't kiss his mother before he goes to bed.

> They all laughed again. Stephen tried to laugh with them. He
> felt his whole body hot and confused in a moment. What was the
> right answer to the question? He had given two and still Wells
> laughed. (*AP*, 14)

There can be no right answer to the question, for either answer is wrong from another viewpoint. The same problem of
choice is posed for Stephen on another level by Dante's maroon
and green brushes:

> He wondered which was right, to be for the green or for the ma-
> roon, because Dante had ripped the green velvet back off the
> brush that was for Parnell one day with her scissors and had told
> him that Parnell was a bad man. He wondered if they were argu-
> ing at home about that. That was called politics. There were two
> sides in it: Dante was on one side and his father and Mr Casey
> were on the other side but his mother and Uncle Charles were on
> no side. (*AP*, 16)

At home, during Christmas, the world of Stephen's family
breaks apart into the "two sides" of this political issue. Again there
is no right answer to Stephen's question. Initially the brush with
the maroon velvet back stood for the Land-leaguer Michael Davitt and the brush with the green velvet back for Parnell, but this
political issue comes to represent an even greater division between
God and the world. When the Church turned against Parnell,
Michael Davitt opposed him. This is the reason Dante ripped off
the green velvet back:

> —God and religion before everything! Dante cried. God and re-
> ligion before the world! Mr Casey raised his clenched fist and
> brought it down on the table with a crash.
> —Very well, then, he shouted hoarsely, if it comes to that, no
> God for Ireland! (*AP*, 39)

From this unresolvable division green will continue throughout the book to suggest Ireland, earth, this life. The maroon color
will become associated with a spiritual realm and Stephen's attempts to transcend this life: "Shrinking from that life he turned
towards the wall, making a cowl of the blanket and staring at the
great overblown scarlet flowers of the tattered wallpaper. He
tried to warm his perishing joy in their scarlet glow, imagining a

roseway from where he lay upwards to heaven all strewn with scarlet flowers" (*AP*, 322). The "green rose," then, that Stephen imagines (*AP*, 7, 12), because it combines these two realms, is an ideal order like that he writes on the flyleaf of his geography book.

The division between God and the world is everywhere encountered in *A Portrait* and ultimately stands behind all of Stephen's unsatisfactory choices. It has already been shown in a detail as small as the anecdote about Stephen's prayer in the wood near Malahide, which comes rather late in the book.

Another appearance of the division in the first chapter is the way Stephen contrasts the smell of the chapel with that of the peasants: "There was a cold night smell in the chapel. But it was a holy smell. It was not like the smell of the old peasants who knelt at the back of the chapel at Sunday mass. That was a smell of air and rain and turf and corduroy" (*AP*, 18). In *Stephen Hero* the smell of the peasants in Clongowes Chapel was thought of by Stephen as "an odour" of "debasing humanity" (*SH*, 238), but here it is a warm, comforting smell that attracts Stephen. He even thinks "it would be lovely to sleep for a night in that cottage before the fire of smoking turf, in the dark lit by the fire, in the warm dark, breathing the smell of the peasants, air and rain and turf and corduroy" (*AP*, 18). Perhaps because this wish suggests a choice that threatens the order of Stephen's world, it contains a danger that frightens him: "But, O, the road there between the trees was dark! You would be lost in the dark. It made him afraid to think of how it was" (*AP*, 18).

Later Stephen will reveal his awareness of this unbridgeable chasm between God and the world in the "heresy" of his essay:

> —Here. It's about the Creator and the soul. Rrm . . . rrm . . . rrm . . . Ah! *without a possibility of ever approaching nearer.* That's heresy.
> Stephen murmured:
> —I meant *without a possibility of ever reaching.* (*AP*, 79)

Because it conceals this rift, the order Stephen reaches at the end of Chapter 1 is soon shattered. Not only does his triumph over Father Dolan prove a deception, but the cosmic chain in the geography book ultimately fails to define Stephen's place.

The first shaking of the order comes from Mr. Dedalus' financial troubles, which prevent Stephen from returning to Clongowes: "For some time he had felt the slight changes in his house; and these changes in what he had deemed unchangeable were so many slight shocks to his boyish conception of the world" (*AP*, 64). His family's move into Dublin further upsets his world: "Dublin was a new and complex sensation" (*AP*, 66). The move is like a dispossession, robbing Stephen of his rightful place in the world. Like the narrator of *Dubliners*, he becomes a detached observer of the squalor around him: "He was angry with himself for being young and the prey of restless foolish impulses, angry also with the change of fortune which was reshaping the world about him into a vision of squalor and insincerity. Yet his anger lent nothing to the vision. He chronicled with patience what he saw, detaching himself from it and tasting its mortifying flavour in secret" (*AP*, 67).

Not only is he divided from the world in this way, but his inner life cannot be made to match the contradictory demands the outer world makes on him:

> While his mind had been pursuing its intangible phantoms and turning in irresolution from such pursuit he had heard about him the constant voices of his father and of his masters, urging him to be a gentleman above all things and urging him to be a good catholic above all things. These voices had now come to be hollow-sounding in his ears. When the gymnasium had been opened he had heard another voice urging him to be strong and manly and healthy and when the movement towards national revival had begun to be felt in the college yet another voice had bidden him to be true to his country and help to raise up her fallen language and tradition. In the profane world, as he foresaw, a worldly voice would bid him raise up his father's fallen state by his labours and, meanwhile, the voice of his school comrades urged him to be a decent fellow, to shield others from blame or to beg them off and to do his best to get free days for the school. And it was the din of all these hollowsounding voices that made him halt irresolutely in pursuit of phantoms. He gave them ear only for a time but he was happy only when he was far from them, beyond their call, alone or in the company of phantasmal comrades. (*AP*, 83–84)

These demands on Stephen are a new form of the either/or riddle. Each voice urges him to choose one thing at the expense of all others. Moreover, they are "hollowsounding" because they fail to coincide with what Stephen perceives to be the reality of the world. For example, his father's advice "to mix with gentlemen" and his claim that "when I was a young fellow . . . I mixed with fine decent fellows (AP, 91) do not seem to match what Stephen knows about him. Instead, the reality of his father's youth is revealed to Stephen by the word he finds carved on a desk in the anatomy theater of his father's college in Cork: "On the desk before him he read the word *Foetus* cut several times in the dark stained wood. The sudden legend startled his blood: he seemed to feel the absent students of the college about him and to shrink from their company. A vision of their life, which his father's words had been powerless to evoke, sprang up before him out of the word cut in the desk" (AP, 90). The vision is detailed and precise, an image of the coarseness of mind that hides behind his father's "fine decent fellows."

The word carved on the desk is troubling to Stephen for another, more important reason. It brings to mind the surest sign of the break in the cosmos, the battle between spirit and flesh: "It shocked him to find in the outer world a trace of what he had deemed till then a brutish and individual malady of his own mind. His recent monstrous reveries came thronging into his memory" (AP, 90). Under the impact of this confrontation, the ordered, hierarchical world finally collapses. Stephen has moved beyond its boundaries: "By his monstrous way of life he seemed to have put himself beyond the limits of reality" (AP, 92). His attempt to hold on to the order and to the identity it gives him is almost a parody of what he had written in his geography book:

> He could scarcely recognize as his own thoughts, and repeated slowly to himself:
> —I am Stephen Dedalus. I am walking beside my father whose name is Simon Dedalus. We are in Cork, in Ireland. Cork is a city. Our room is in the Victoria Hotel. Victoria and Stephen and Simon. Simon and Stephen and Victoria. Names.
> The memory of his childhood suddenly grew dim. He tried to call forth some of its vivid moments but could not. (AP, 92–93)

The experience is like that of his sickness at Clongowes and his dream of being dead: "He had not died but he had faded out like a film in the sun. He had been lost or had wandered out of existence for he no longer existed. How strange to think of him passing out of existence in such a way, not by death but by fading out in the sun or by being lost and forgotten somewhere in the universe!" (*AP*, 93). Stephen's inability to find a relationship between his inner feelings and desires and the life of those around him forces an even greater separation from them. There is no connection between the kind of lust for contact he feels and what seems to be the life of his family. This failure is another sign of the division between spirit and matter on which Stephen's universe breaks apart.

Caught in this break Stephen seems to view the life of other people from a high, indifferent vantage point, reminiscent of the narrator's position in *Dubliners*:

> Stephen watched the three glasses being raised from the counter as his father and his two cronies drank to the memory of their past. An abyss of fortune or of temperament sundered him from them. His mind seemed older than theirs: it shone coldly on their strifes and happiness and regrets like a moon upon a younger earth. No life or youth stirred in him as it had stirred in them. . . . Nothing stirred within his soul but a cold and cruel and loveless lust. His childhood was dead or lost and with it his soul capable of simple joys, and he was drifting amid life like the barren shell of the moon. (*AP*, 96)

The lines of Shelley he remembers suggest precisely the break in the universe which his own separation from the world indicates:

> *Art thou pale for weariness*
> *Of climbing heaven and gazing on the earth,*
> *Wandering companionless . . . ?*

> He repeated to himself the lines of Shelley's fragment. Its alternation of sad human ineffectualness with vast inhuman cycles of activity chilled him, and he forgot his own human and ineffectual grieving. (*AP*, 96)

If his own isolation is merely a symptom of a vast cosmic disorder, perhaps there is nothing he can do to mitigate it. Perhaps he must try to live the illusory life of other people, ignoring his isolation. Perhaps he must accept the alienation of his outer and inner life.

With prize money from an essay contest Stephen tries to impose an order on his life, to draw near to his family, and to live outwardly as his society wants him to do. He even draws up "a form of commonwealth for the household" in which every member of the family holds some office. It is a parody of a social order that exists on the surface of some great disorder and the life of the ordinary man who skims along that surface, ignoring the rift it thinly covers. This attempt at order also fails:

> How foolish his aim had been! He had tried to build a break-water of order and elegance against the sordid tide of life without him and to dam up, by rules of conduct and active interests and new filial relations, the powerful recurrence of the tides within him. Useless. From without as from within the water had flowed over his barriers: their tides began once more to jostle fiercely above the crumbled mole.
>
> He saw clearly too his own futile isolation. He had not gone one step nearer the lives he had sought to approach nor bridged the restless shame and rancour that divided him from mother and brother and sister. (*AP*, 98)

The pressure that comes from within Stephen and demands to be released is the experience of his own body, and it demands a release that is not sanctioned by the social and religious order that rules his world. Not only does it demand a break in Stephen's normal relationship with the world, but also, since it demands contact with another person, it is pressure toward an encounter which violates the self. The demand of his body is in itself experienced as a clash with otherness that underlines the division already existing in Stephen's world and in his being: "He felt some dark presence subtle and murmurous as a flood filling him wholly with itself. Its murmur besieged his ears like the murmur of some multitude in sleep; its subtle streams penetrated his being. His hands clenched convulsively and his teeth set together as he suffered the agony of its penetration" (*AP*, 100). When he finally wanders into the "maze of narrow and dirty streets" (*AP*, 100) of the brothel district, he is described as awakening in another world (*AP*, 100), and his first contact with a prostitute is described in terms of a penetration of the self, like those other encounters with reality: "He closed his eyes, surrendering himself to her, body and mind, conscious of nothing in the world but the dark pressure of her softly parting lips. They pressed upon his brain as upon his lips as though they were the vehicle of a vague speech; and between them he felt an unknown and timid pressure, darker than the swoon of sin, softer than sound or odour" (*AP*, 101).

Stephen's encounter here is an unforeseen fulfillment, though only a partial one, of his desire to "meet in the real world the unsubstantial image which his soul so constantly beheld" (*AP*, 65). The desire had its source in a fantasy about a romantic "Mercedes" who would mate the soul of the lonely boy: "a premonition which led him on told him that this image would, without any overt act of his, encounter him" (*AP*, 65). The "unrest" which is the source of the fantasy (*AP*, 66), however, is the sign of his feeling of incompleteness. Stephen's search for the fantasy girl and "the holy encounter at which weakness and timidity and inexperience were to fall from him" (*AP*, 99) leads him on his long walks through the streets of Dublin and eventually into the brothel district. "The vastness and strangeness of the life . . . wakened again in him the unrest which had sent him wandering in the evening from garden to garden in search of Mercedes. . . . A vague dissatisfaction grew up within him as he looked on the quays and on the river and on the lowering skies and yet he continued to wander up and down day after day as if he really sought someone that eluded him" (*AP*, 66).

Dorothy Van Ghent in the essay cited above has called attention to the importance of the walking motif in *A Portrait* as a manifestation of Stephen's inner movement through chaos to a new order. Miss Van Ghent describes the motif in this way: Stephen's "ambulatory movements take him into new localities, among new impressions, as his mind moves correspondingly into new spiritual localities that subsume the older ones and readjust them as parts of a larger whole" (p. 271).

Mircea Eliade has discussed the mythical and symbolic reverberations of the motif of walking in a way that makes use of the details of Stephen's condition and of his search:

> Even the most habitual gesture can signify a spiritual act. The road and walking can be transfigured into religious values, for

every road can symbolize the "road of life," and any walk a "pilgrimage," a peregrination to the Center of the World. If possessing a house implies having assumed a stable situation in the world, those who have renounced their houses, the pilgrims and ascetics, proclaim by their "walking," by their constant movement, their desire to leave the world, their refusal of any worldly situation. . . . Those who have chosen the Quest, the road that leads to the Center, must abandon any kind of family and social situation, any "nest," and devote themselves wholly to "walking" toward the supreme truth, which, in highly evolved religions, is synonymous with the Hidden God, the *Deus absconditus*.[4]

Stephen's search already has led him to break with home and family. As it ends in exile, it will finally lead him to break with the established church and his country: in short, to a "refusal of any worldly situation." Like the quest for the *Deus absconditus* of which Eliade speaks, Stephen's search is for a "holy encounter," an instant of union with otherness, that will transfigure him and his world. Eliade's description captures the way Stephen himself would think of his wandering. His quest ends, however, in ways that he does not expect and which do not fit Eliade's scheme. Instead of Eliade's division between sacred and profane, Joyce's solution will ultimately be to find the sacred in the profane world. In *Ulysses* Stephen's quest will bring him home again, to a new family situation. Even here in *A Portrait* Stephen's search brings him to the prostitute.

He imagines his tryst with Mercedes in this way: "They would be alone, surrounded by darkness and silence: and in that moment of supreme tenderness he would be transfigured. He would fade into something impalpable under her eyes and then in a moment, he would be transfigured. Weakness and timidity and inexperience would fall from him in that magic moment" (*AP*, 65). This hope seems for a moment to be realized in the arms not of Mercedes but of the prostitute: "In her arms he felt that he had suddenly become strong and fearless and sure of himself" (*AP*, 101).

Still, this attempt at contact with otherness does not solve Stephen's problem of the separation between self and world. Like his answer to Wells's question, it is the forced choice of an inadequate solution. Although it is an advance in experience, Stephen's choice of the flesh not only leaves the spirit unsatisfied, it debases it. This encounter and the ones that follow it intensify the split in his world and his separation from other people. His immersion in a reality that he finds spiritually debasing is again described in terms not unlike the realism of the *Dubliners* narrator: "Yet as he prowled in quest of that call, his senses, stultified only by his desire, would note keenly all that wounded or shamed them; his eyes, a ring of porter froth on a clothless table or a photograph of two soldiers standing at attention or a gaudy playbill; his ears, the drawling jargon of greeting" (*AP*, 102). By choosing flesh, Stephen only obtains momentary satisfaction, a temporary "dark peace" (*AP*, 103) between body and soul. His world is just as divided as it ever was.

Actually because Stephen has chosen to divide the world and live only a partial answer to his needs, the result can never be satisfactory to him: "His soul was fattening and congealing into a gross grease, plunging ever deeper in its dull fear into a sombre threatening dusk, while the body that was his stood, listless and dishonoured, gazing out of darkened eyes, helpless, perturbed and human for a bovine god to stare upon" (*AP*, 111).

Stephen's return to the church, a choice for the spirit, is just as unsatisfactory, but it also requires at first the breakdown of the wall of the self. The words of Father Arnall's sermons during the retreat merge with Stephen's thoughts and become his words. His return to the faith requires his confession, which is both a release from isolation and something like a death for the ego: "To say it in words! His soul, stifling and helpless, would cease to be" (*AP*, 142). Again, he passes outside the limits of the world into a nothingness and returns once more in the imagery of an awakening: "One soul was lost; a tiny soul: his. It flickered once and went out, forgotten, lost. The end: black cold void waste. Consciousness of place came ebbing back to him slowly over a vast tract of time unlit, unfelt, unlived. The squalid scene composed itself around him" (*AP*, 141).

After his confession, the world seems fresh and ordered again: "On the dresser was a plate of sausages and white pudding and on the shelf there were eggs. They would be for the breakfast in the morning after the communion in the college chapel. White pudding and eggs and sausages and cups of tea. How simple and beautiful was life after all! And life lay all before him" (*AP*, 146). The Miltonic echo in the last phrase is quite appropriate, not only because the repentant Stephen is beginning a new life, but also because it suggests that this life will be something less than a paradise regained.

The new life that Stephen has chosen is not at all life in a fallen world. In fact, "the world for all its solid substance and complexity no longer existed for his soul save as a theorem of a divine power and love and universality. So entire and unquestionable was this sense of the divine meaning in all nature granted to his soul that he could scarcely understand why it was in any way necessary that he should continue to live" (*AP*, 150). That this new order maintains the old split in the world is revealed by the fact that Stephen's regimen of the spirit requires a mortification of the flesh and senses (*AP*, 150–51). The more he tries to escape the world, however, the more he is called back to it by the most irritatingly insignificant things: "It surprised him however to find at the end of his course of intricate piety and selfrestraint he was so easily at the mercy of childish and unworthy imperfections. His prayers and fasts availed him little for the suppression of anger at hearing his mother sneeze or at being disturbed in his devotions" (*AP*, 151).

Stephen is as isolated from others as he ever was; moreover, the connection he felt with a transcendent world begins to weaken. In spiritual pride, he has toyed with old temptations: "When he had eluded the flood of temptation many times . . . he grew troubled and wondered whether the grace which he had refused to lose was not being filched from him little by little. The clear certitude of his own immunity grew dim and to it succeeded a vague fear that his soul had really fallen unawares" (*AP*, 152–53). Stephen's doubts grow out of the distance that exists between the spiritual realm and the earth. His lack of certainty and the feeling of the dissipation of grace are the signs of the chasm which his decision has done nothing to bridge.

Furthermore, past sins keep coming back to haunt him. At his communion he seemed a new man, facing a new life: "The past

was past" (*AP*, 140). It turns out, however, that he has not escaped
the world. In his condition he has nothing to report to his confessor
except such minor imperfections as anger at his mother's sneezing:

> Often when he had confessed his doubts and scruples, some mo-
> mentary inattention at prayer, a movement of trivial anger in his
> soul or a subtle wilfulness in speech or act, he was bidden by his
> confessor to name some sin of his past life before absolution was
> given him. He named it with humility and shame and repented
> of it once more. It humiliated and shamed him to think that he
> would never be freed from it wholly, however holily he might live
> or whatever virtues or perfections he might attain. A restless feel-
> ing of guilt would always be present with him: he would confess
> and repent and be absolved, confess and repent again and be
> absolved again, fruitlessly. (*AP*, 153)

Again, the order Stephen attempts to impose on his world falls
apart.

At first it seems that his decision to live out the prophecy of his
name in the creation of art offers a new hope: "This was the call
of life to his soul not the dull gross voice of the world of duties
and despair, not the inhuman voice that had called him to the
pale service of the altar" (*AP*, 169). This new possibility seems to
unite body and spirit: "His soul was soaring in an air beyond the
world and the body he knew was purified in a breath and deliv-
ered of incertitude and made radiant and commingled with the
element of the spirit" (*AP*, 69). It is another moment of ecstasy
which echoes the fantasized tryst with Mercedes and the encounter with the prostitute "at which weakness and timidity and inexperience were to fall from him" (*AP*, 99). The established pattern
would suggest that this flight would lead to another fall. In fact,
the prophecy of the fall accompanies the flight. Stephen's ecstatic
revery is interrupted by the cries of boys in the water:

> —One! Two! . . . Look out!
> —O, cripes, I'm drownded! (*AP*, 169)

Stephen's flight is still an attempt to get beyond the world. In
this new attempt at order Stephen will become even more separated from the lives of those around him: "You're a terrible man,

Stevie . . . always alone," Davin tells him (*AP*, 201). In the name of art and self (*AP*, 247) Stephen spurns family, religion, and nation and goes into exile. But among his fears is not the fear of failure. As I said earlier, it is almost as if having grasped the rhythmic pattern of his experience, Stephen wills the fall that he must suffer: "To live, to err, to fail, to triumph, to recreate life out of life!" (*AP*, 172). For Stephen, then, in this novel the solution to the problem of his relationship with the world lies in his commitment to art. It is almost as if Joyce has come full circle from the early stories. The point Stephen has reached and the point at which *Dubliners* began seem to coincide.

What has happened, then, to the resolution found at the end of "The Dead"? It is true that Stephen has reached the same position as the narrator at the beginning of *Dubliners*. The hidden structure of that book and of *Stephen Hero* has come to the surface in *A Portrait*. Stephen's exile is the realization of his spiritual condition of separation from the other. He has become a detached observer of life. The diary he is keeping at the end of the novel, as William York Tindall has pointed out, is the symbol of his egocentricity.[5] Stephen's final solution in *A Portrait* is another doomed attempt to escape. The narrator of *A Portrait* is not a disguised version of Stephen, however, as he was in *Stephen Hero*. The divided structure of the observer and observed is held together by a narrator who represents both sides of this dualism. The form of *A Portrait* itself denies the rift that seems to exist in Stephen's world.

The subjectivism of the form has often been described. The reader sees, hears, knows nothing that has not been filtered through Stephen's mind. The narrator's words themselves are styled by the stage of Stephen's consciousness: for example, the short, choppy sentences of the first chapter which suggest the naive mind of the child; the religious rhetoric of the third chapter; the Paterian imagery at the end of the fourth chapter when Stephen sees the girl on the beach. This union of Stephen and the narrator is unlike the secret agreement between a supposedly objective narrator and his subject in *Stephen Hero*.

Although he has made himself the interpreter of Stephen's vision, the narrator of *A Portrait* does not corroborate that vision.

The world in Stephen's mind always exceeds his understanding of
it in a way that is apparent to the reader even when it is not to
Stephen. Stephen himself is aware of this fact at one point:
"Masked memories passed quickly before him: he recognized
scenes and persons yet he was conscious that he failed to perceive
some vital circumstance in them" (*AP*, 157). The presence of the
narrator, however, often alerts the reader to that vital circumstance which Stephen misses. For example, when Stephen's mind
soars upwards in flight, the reader's attention is deflected down-
wards by the cry of the boy in the water: "O, cripes, I'm
drownded!" (*AP*, 169). In that same scene, Stephen seems to hear
a voice calling him from beyond the world:

> Again! Again! Again! A voice from beyond the world was calling.
> —Hello, Stephanos!
> —Here comes The Dedalus! (*AP*, 167)

It is, however, only his friends calling to him from what he fears
most, the water: "The mere sight of that medley of wet nakedness
chilled him to the bone. . . . But he, apart from them and in silence, remembered in what dread he stood of the mystery of his
own body" (*AP*, 168). The water, associated here with the body,
is also the fluidity of life and the imagination (*AP*, 172, 215), and
the breakdown of the barriers of the self is usually accompanied
by the imagery of flooding (*AP*, 98, 103, 152–53).

Stephen's reveries are constantly being broken by the intrusion
of a reality which complements or counters them but always provides a link between his inner and outer lives. The awakening to
a world of noises and things is one of the most common motifs in
the book:

> All the people. Welcome home, Stephen! Noises of welcome.
> His mother kissed him. Was that right? His father was a marshall
> now: higher than a magistrate. Welcome home, Stephen!
> Noises . . .
> There was a noise of curtainrings running back along the rods,
> of water being splashed in the basins. There was a noise of rising
> and dressing and washing in the dormitory: a noise of clapping of
> hands as the prefect went up and down telling the fellows to look

sharp. A pale sunlight showed the yellow curtains drawn back, the tossed beds. (*AP*, 20–21; see also 100, 141, 146, 173, 217, 218, 221)

Stephen is called back to reality by such things as a word carved in a desk that suddenly connects his secret thoughts with the lives of others (*AP*, 89–90), by his mother's sneezing (*AP*, 149), by the hard and sudden speech of a flower girl who innocently mimics his fantasy (*AP*, 183–84, 220). Even the poem Stephen writes, the "Villanelle of the Temptress," is concerned with this theme. It is about the seduction of seraphim by a temptress who is E.C., the worldly woman, one of the symbols of Ireland (*AP*, 221), and the archetype of all those girls, such as the flower girl, who call to Stephen in the street (*AP*, 220). Stephen naturally is the seraph— "In a dream or vision he had known the ecstasy of seraphic life" (*AP*, 217). The dream is appropriate because it coincides with his waking dream of angelism. The poem is another instance of the fall into reality.

The order that Stephen imposes on his experience is most often an aesthetic order. What is a crucial motif in this book anticipates the structure of *Ulysses*. In *A Portrait* Stephen perceives reality, understands his experiences according to some art model or other. In *Ulysses* the model—journalism, the saga, the dime novel, the fugue—is a given of the form.

In Chapter 5 of *A Portrait*, Stephen has a model for each stage of his walk toward University College:

> The rainladen trees of the avenue evoked in him, as always, memories of the girls and women in the plays of Gerhart Hauptmann; and the memory of their pale sorrows and the fragrance falling from the wet branches mingled in a mood of quiet joy. His morning walk across the city had begun, and he foreknew that as he passed the sloblands of Fairview he would think of the cloistral silverveined prose of Newman, that as he walked along the North Strand Road, glancing idly at the windows of the provision shops, he would recall the dark humour of Guido Cavalcanti and smile, that as he went by Baird's stonecutting works in Talbot Place the spirit of Ibsen would blow through him like a keen wind, a spirit of wayward boyish beauty, and that passing a grimy marine-

dealer's shop beyond the Liffey he would repeat the song by Ben
Jonson which begins:
I was not wearier where I lay. (*AP*, 176)

Earlier in his religious phase, painting provided one of his models:
"The attitude of rapture in sacred art, the raised and parted
hands, the parted lips and eyes as of one about to swoon, became
for him an image of the soul in prayer, humiliated and faint before her Creator" (*AP*, 150). In addition, his spiritual communions
with the Blessed Sacrament are in the mode of "an old neglected
book written by saint Alphonsus Liguori, with fading characters
and sere foxpapered leaves" (*AP*, 152). In Chapter 3 Father Arnall's sermon becomes reality for Stephen. The sermon has such a
powerful sway over Stephen's imagination that the distance between his thoughts and Father Arnall's words is collapsed. Stephen thinks the sermon and lives the sermon. In Chapter 2, the
form and title of Stephen's verses to E.C. are modelled after the
collected poems of Lord Byron. "The unsubstantial image which
his soul so constantly beheld" and which Stephen seeks to meet in
"the real world" is the image of Mercedes from a "ragged translation of The Count of Monte Cristo" (*AP*, 62, 65).

Everywhere and always Stephen's reality is mediated by literature. His experience is already an imitation of art rather than
the reverse. The book begins "Once upon a time . . . ," and Stephen's first action is to find himself and his experience in the story
his father told him: "He was baby tuckoo. The moocow came
down the road where Betty Byrne lived" (*AP*, 7).

The word is primary for Stephen. Life is always and already
language. On his way to University College he is said to walk "in
a lane among heaps of dead language" (*AP*, 179). By means of
language, already present language, Stephen is able to apprehend
reality, that is to say, whatever exists outside language. "Words
which he did not understand he said over and over to himself till
he had learned them by heart: and through them he had glimpses
of the real world about him" (*AP*, 62). Toward the end of Chapter
4, when Stephen whispered to himself the phrase "A day of dap-
pled seaborne clouds," "the phrase and the day and the scene har-
monized in a chord" (*AP*, 166). The quotidian reality, however,

is founded upon language that is dead, received ideas. This concept is the basis for the parodies in the forms of the various episodes of *Ulysses*. It is the task of the artist to expose the received structure of reality and to create a new reality, to transmute "the daily bread of experience into the radiant body of everliving life." It is because life imitates art that Stephen and Joyce can hope to create "the conscience"—consciousness—of their race.

There is still another way that the form of *A Portrait* denies the separation between Stephen and his world. The organization of *Stephen Hero* separated Stephen from an external time and yet showed his secret dependence on the passing of time. *A Portrait* is made up of a series of discontinuous, present moments which exist in Stephen's mind. In the present moments Stephen's situation brings into focus relevant moments from the past and premonitions of the future; in Stephen's words, "the past is consumed in the present and the present is living only because it brings forth the future" (*AP*, 251). As many critics have pointed out, the basic elements are the same in each of these moments although these elements are always rearranged into a new relationship with each other at each appearance. Professor Ellmann accounts for this characteristic when he reports that "the book's pattern, as . . . [Joyce] explained to Stanislaus, is that we are what we were; our maturity is an extension of our childhood, and the courageous boy is father of the arrogant young man" (*JJ*, 306).

Joyce's early essay version of *A Portrait* also suggests his intentions with this method: "The features of infancy are not commonly reproduced in the adolescent portrait for, so capricious are we, that we cannot or will not conceive the past in any other than its iron memorial aspect. Yet the past assuredly implies a fluid succession of presents, the development of an entity of which our actual present is a phase only" (*Workshop*, 60). There are some artists, he continued, "who seek through some art, by some process of the mind as yet untabulated, to liberate from the personalised lumps of matter that which is their individuating rhythm, the first or formal relation of their parts. But for such as these a portrait is not an identificative paper but rather the curve of an emotion" (*Workshop*, 60).[6] Each chapter of *A Portrait* is a "succession of presents," of a developing being. By this means the narrator builds up a serial "portrait" of Stephen's "individuating rhythm" or "curve of an emotion" which is a cyclical ascent and fall. Each chapter, then, is an image of the whole which is also a series of the separate chapters. Because each of these "parts" (present moment, chapter, book) repeats Stephen's "individuating rhythm," Stephen's whole being is present in each moment. Scholes and Kain cite a passage from Walter Pater's essay on Giorgione as a contributing source of Stephen's theory of the epiphany, but the passage seems more relevant to the organization of A *Portrait*:

> Now it is part of the ideality of the highest sort of dramatic poetry, that it presents us with a kind of profoundly significant and. animated instants . . . some brief and wholly concrete moment—into which, however, all the motives, all the interests and effects of a long history, have condensed themselves, and which seem to absorb past and future in an intense consciousness of the present. Such ideal instants the school of Giorgione selects, with its admirable tact, from that feverish, tumultuously colored world of the old citizens of Venice—exquisite pauses in time, in which, arrested thus, we seem to be spectators of all the fullness of existence, and which are like some consummate extract or quintessence of life. (*Workshop*, 257–58)

Each of these arrested "moments" in this "portrait" of Stephen represents "all the fullness of existence." Yet each moment, like "Cranly's way of remembering thoughts in connection with places" (*AP*, 245), connects Stephen's mind with a particular time and place. Each moment reveals Stephen wholly present in the world from which he feels separated, reflecting it as it reflects him. A portrait of Stephen is simultaneously a portrait of his world and of him in it.

Stephen will come to an awareness of his inescapable relationship to his world in the early hours of June 17, 1904, in the Dublin kitchen of Leopold Bloom, when he affirms "his significance as . . . a conscious rational reagent between a micro- and macrocosm ineluctably constructed upon the incertitude of the void" (*U*, 697). In a letter to H. L. Mencken in July of 1915, Joyce spoke of *Ulysses* as "a continuation of *A Portrait of the Artist* and also of *Dubliners*" (*Letters*, I, 83). In *Dubliners*, Joyce had attempted an objective, external picture of the city. *A Portrait* is the inner life of a young boy growing up in Dublin. *Ulysses* brings these two poles and their methods together in a way that is only implicit in the ending of "The Dead" and in *A Portrait*.

NOTES

1. For explanation of the markings in passages from *Stephen Hero*, see p. 22, n. 5.
2. Dorothy Van Ghent, *The English Novel: Form and Function* (New York: Rinehart, 1959), pp. 270 ff. Further references to this book will be identified in the text. See also Hugh Kenner's "The Portrait in Perspective," in *James Joyce: Two Decades of Criticism*, ed. Seon Givens (New York: The Vanguard Press, 1963), p. 169, and the same essay in a slightly different form in Kenner's *Dublin's Joyce*, pp. 122, 129.
3. I am grateful to Dr. Edgar A. Dryden for calling my attention to these prayers and to Stephen's hierarchically ordered universe. Many of the ideas in this chapter were developed in conversations with him, and his criticisms of this study have proved very useful to me.
4. *The Sacred and the Profane*, trans. Willard R. Trask (New York: Harper Torchbooks, 1961), pp. 183–84.
5. *A Reader's Guide to James Joyce* (New York: The Noonday Press, 1959), p. 69.
6. For an explication of Joyce's aesthetic of the "rhythmic gesture" see Jackson I. Cope, "The Rhythmic Gesture: Image and Aesthetic in Joyce's *Ulysses*," *ELH*, 29 (March, 1962), 67–89, esp. pp. 67–74.

Epilogue: The Dublin Peer Gynt
and the Fate of the Egoist

THE OUTCOME of Stephen Dedalus' quest for self in *Ulysses* is clarified by Joyce's early plans to make that book a Dublin *Peer Gynt*. Richard Ellmann has reported that during the autumn of 1907, shortly after finishing "The Dead" and beginning *A Portrait*, Joyce began to think again about the story he planned to write entitled "Ulysses":

> On November 10 Stanislaus noted in his diary: "Jim told me that he is going to expand his story 'Ulysses' into a short book and make a Dublin 'Peer Gynt' of it. I think that some suggestions of mine put him in the way of making it important. As it happens in one day, I suggested that he should make a comedy of it, but he won't. It should be good." . . . In what sense *Ulysses* was to be a *Peer Gynt* is not altogether clear, except that the hero was to sample all aspects of Dublin life. How he could be at once the clear-eyed Ulysses and the self-deceived Peer Gynt is also unexplained. (*JJ*, 275)

But the conjunction of this idea with Joyce's new plans for *A Portrait* suggests that he was already considering *Ulysses* as a sequel[1] and it is no longer Ibsen the realist who is Joyce's model but the vastly different Ibsen of *Peer Gynt*. It is the egoist Stephen, not Bloom, that Joyce was thinking of as a Peer Gynt.

Like Stephen, Peer is born into the world dispossessed and disinherited. His father has wasted his inheritance, just as Stephen's

132

father has done. Like Stephen, Peer does battle with the Trolls
and then goes into exile. In Ibsen's play the Trolls suggest the Nor-
wegian nationalists. They represent a radical selfishness and a destructive kind of self-sufficiency. As the Old Man, King of the
Trolls, explains it:

> Among men the saying goes: "Man be thyself!"
> At home here with us, 'mid the tribe of the trolls,
> The saying goes: "Troll to thyself be—enough!"[2]

The name of the Irish nationalist group, the Sinn Fein, means in
English, coincidentally, "Ourselves Alone." Joyce had applied the
word "trolls" to the Irish public in his 1901 essay "The Day of the
Rabblement" (CW, 71).[3]

Both Stephen and Peer are obsessed with the idea of truly being
themselves at the expense of everything and everyone else. When
asked to define the nature of the Gyntish self, Peer says:

> The world behind my forehead's arch,
> By force of which I'm no one else
> Than I, no more than God's the Devil.
> (IV.i., p. 176)

Stephen has also tried to purge the self of all external claims and
influences with his "non serviam," escaping the nets of God, country, and family. Perhaps it is possible to read Joyce's intentions
concerning the fate of Stephen in what happens to Peer Gynt.

After giving up every evidence of his selfishness, Peer is astonished when upon returning from exile he is accused of having
failed in his quest for self. He is met by "The Button-moulder,"
who has orders from "The Master" to melt Peer down for recast-
ing because he has failed to be himself. Peer is confounded. If he
hasn't been himself, what has he been? In Ulysses, Stephen has
returned from exile to confront more indefinite but hardly less profound doubts about himself.

The Button-moulder gives Peer a brief reprieve to seek out witnesses to his steadfastness in being Peer. The first man he happens
upon is the Old Man, King of the Trolls. Peer wants the Old
Man to testify to his fight to avoid being branded as a Troll, as

evidence of how thoroughly he had remained himself. The Old Man, however, cannot testify to this and reveals that Peer actually had been branded with the Troll motto—"To thyself be enough" —and had lived as a Troll all those years. Peer has become the very opposite of what he thought he was and the image of what he most hated and feared. As much as Stephen has tried to free himself from his environment and found his self on a denial of Dublin, he too has not escaped. He too belongs to what he hated and feared.

It appears that the satanic project of self-creation is an impossibility, that becoming oneself is founded upon a paradox. When Peer again meets the Button-moulder, he asks him just "what is it, at bottom, this 'being oneself'?" The Button-moulder answers:

> To be oneself is: to slay oneself.
> But on you that answer is doubtless lost;
> And therefore we'll say: to stand forth everywhere
> With Master's intention displayed like a sign-board.
> (V.ix., pp. 301–2)

To fulfill one's destiny, as Stephen has pledged to do, the idea of self must be sacrificed. To become oneself, one must die to the self.

Peer is granted one more reprieve, this time to prove that he has been a great sinner. Even that would be some proof that he had been himself. In final desperation he seizes upon Solveig, his deserted wife, to give this evidence, but she refuses. He is lost, he cries, unless she can answer the riddle of his existence:

> PEER
> Canst thou tell where Peer Gynt has been since we parted?
> SOLVEIG
> Been?
> PEER
> With his destiny's seal on his brow;
> Been, as in God's thought he first sprang forth!
> Canst thou tell me? If not, I must get me home,—
> Go down to the mist-shrouded regions.

SOLVEIG

[*Smiling*]

Oh, that riddle is easy.

PEER

Then tell what thou knowest!

Where was I, as myself, as the whole man, the trueman?

Where was I, with God's sigil upon my brow?

SOLVEIG

In my faith, in my hope, and in my love.

(V.x., pp. 319–20)

Peer is saved. The Archers footnote that last line to reveal that what they have translated as "love" is the word *Kjaerlighed*, which actually means "charity" in the biblical sense. Faith, hope, and charity toward the other. Although Leopold Bloom is the unlikeliest Solveig imaginable, such also is Stephen's salvation. Stephen discovers himself in the spirit of the other. The image of the alienated observer is transcended. Stephen is a part of all he sees. In *Ulysses*, Stephen will discover that "we walk through ourselves, meeting robbers, ghosts, giants, old men, young men, wives, widows, brothers-in-love. But always meeting ourselves."

NOTES

1. There is, of course, no certainty that Stephen was in Joyce's original plans for the *Dubliners* story. Professor Ellmann, however, believes that the action of the story remains in the novel *Ulysses*. Recently he reviewed the evidence ("Odyssey of a Unique Book," *New York Times Magazine*, November 14, 1965, p. 56). Joyce's "Ulysses" was originally based on a Dubliner named Alfred Hunter whom Joyce knew only slightly: "Joyce had met Hunter in ignominious circumstances. As far as the incident can be pieced together from the talk of family and friends, Joyce was dead drunk one night in Dublin's brothel district and was knocked down in a fight. From this predicament Hunter, a man he had met only once or twice, rescued him. Hunter was rumored to be Jewish and to have an unfaithful wife, two disparate points that became crucial later" ("Odyssey," p. 56). These details, Ellmann believes, would have formed the

story Joyce planned for *Dubliners*. He claims that "the story would describe Hunter's peripatetic journey through Dublin, and presumably it would conclude with his rescue of a young man resembling Joyce from a nasty situation" ("Odyssey," p. 56). The possibilities for a symmetry that Joyce favored are intriguing, for a story of this sort would have paralleled the unidentified young man's "rescue" of the unconscious Mr. Kernan at the beginning of "Grace."

Still, there is no indication that the young man whom Hunter was to rescue in the story would be identified as Stephen Dedalus. There is, however, another clue. In 1917 Joyce told Georges Borach that "in Rome when I had finished about half the *Portrait*, I realized that the Odyssey had to be the sequel, and I began to write *Ulysses*" (*JJ*, 430). It was, of course, still *Stephen Hero* that Joyce was working on while he was in Rome and he is undoubtedly referring to the story "Ulysses" as the beginning of his later novel. But the suggestion is that as soon as he had conceived of the story he began to think of it as the completion of Stephen's story. It is even possible that the reason he did not use the idea for *Dubliners* was that he saw Stephen as a necessary part of it.

At any rate, Joyce's announcement of his plans to make *Ulysses* "a Dublin 'Peer Gynt' " came at the moment he had begun to transform *Stephen Hero* into *A Portrait*, and it seems likely that he had Stephen in mind at that time. The resemblances between Stephen and Peer, as discussed in this section, strengthen this likelihood.

The dividing point between *A Portrait* and *Ulysses* was probably a late decision on Joyce's part. There are pages from an apparently late manuscript version of *A Portrait* which combine material Joyce used in *A Portrait* with material near the beginning of Ulysses. For these, see *Workshop*, 106–8, and for an analysis of these fragments, A. Walton Litz, *The Art of James Joyce: Method and Design in* Ulysses *and* Finnegans Wake (New York: Oxford Galaxy Book, 1964), Appendix D, pp. 132–41.

2. Henrik Ibsen, *The Works of Henrik Ibsen*, Vol. 4, *Peer Gynt: A Dramatic Poem*, trans. William and Charles Archer (New York: Charles Scribner's Sons, 1911), II.vi., p. 112. Further quotations from *Peer Gynt* in my text will be from this edition, but will be identified by act and scene, as well as page number in this edition, to facilitate reference to other translations. Joyce may have bought the English version of this edition between October, 1913, and May, 1914, during the late stages of his composition of *A Portrait*; see *JJ*, 788. The fact that he purchased some edition of the play during this

period, even though he had known the play in the original for some time, suggests that his idea about relating *Ulysses* to it was still alive.

3. See also *JJ*, 93, 181, for Joyce's early idea of "trolls."

Index

Abbreviations are explained on pages xi-xii

139

This book was set in eleven-point Caledonia and printed by
Oberlin Printing Company, Oberlin, Ohio.
It was bound by John H. Dekker & Sons, Inc., Grand Rapids, Michigan.
The book was designed by LaWanda J. McDuffie.